The Witches' Almanac

Spring 2023 — Spring 2024

CONTAINING pictorial and explicit delineations of the
magical phases of the Moon together with information about astrological
portents of the year to come and various aspects of occult knowledge
enabling all who read to improve their lives in the old manner.

The Witches' Almanac, Ltd.

Publishers   Providence, Rhode Island
www.TheWitchesAlmanac.com

Address all inquiries and information to
THE WITCHES' ALMANAC, LTD.
P.O. Box 25239
Providence, RI   02905-7700

13-ISBN: 978-1-881098-88-1 The Witches' Almanac—Classic
13-ISBN: 978-1-881098-87-4 The Witches' Almanac—Standard
E-Book 13-ISBN: 978-1-881098-89-8 The Witches' Almanac—Standard

ISSN: 1522-3184

First Printing July 2022

Printed in USA

Established 1971 by Elizabeth Pepper

Preface

Power is power; the power to create, the power to sustain, the power to transform, power to be yourself—inside and out.

Witches are inherently part of our environment, both in thought and in truth. We must not go through life blindly following, but rather we should lead. We need to express our passions to fulfill our dreams. This is what will take humanity to new levels. Following the crowd only causes stagnation. The inertia of stagnation hinders the progress of evolution.

Power comes from our decision and our actions. Witches act. We are not complacent.

When an important decision is made, it should be done from the heart, only secondarily from the mind.

From the heart—search. Search every nook and cranny of your soul to KNOW that your decision is true. Unless you have done this, you need not encourage others to follow your suggestion or actions. If you want to be a leader, you need to have full conviction. And, full conviction does not give consent to change your mind. You can adjust your thinking when new information becomes available. But solid conviction does not come from knowledge. It comes from wisdom.

Search your soul. Know your ideals. Act on your principles.

The opposite of power is nothing.

❧ HOLIDAYS ❧

Spring 2023 to Spring 2024

March 20, 2023 . . . . Vernal Equinox
April 1 . . . . All Fools' Day
April 8 . . . . Vesak Day
April 30 . . . . Walpurgis Night
May 1 . . . . Beltane
May 8 . . . . White Lotus Day
May 29 . . . . Oak Apple Day
June 5 . . . . Night of the Watchers
June 21 . . . . Summer Solstice
June 24 . . . . Midsummer
July 23 . . . . Ancient Egyptian New Year
July 31 . . . . Lughnassad Eve
August 1 . . . . Lammas
August 13 . . . . Diana's Day
August 17 . . . . Black Cat Appreciation Day
Setember 18 . . . . Ganesh Chaturthi
September 23 . . . . Autumnal Equinox
October 31 . . . . Samhain Eve
November 1 . . . . Hallowmas
November 16 . . . . Hecate Night
December 16 . . . . Fairy Queen Eve
December 17 . . . . Saturnalia
December 21 . . . . Winter Solstice
January 9, 2024 . . . . Feast of Janus
February 1 . . . . Oimelc Eve
February 2 . . . . Candlemas
February 10 . . . . Chinese New Year
February 15 . . . . Lupercalia
March 1 . . . . Matronalia
March 19 . . . . Minerva's Day

Art Director . . . . Gwion Vran

Astrologer . . . . Dikki-Jo Mullen

Climatologist . . . . Tom C. Lang

Cover Art and Design. . . . Kathryn Sky-Peck

Sales . . . . Roy Singleton

Bookkeeping . . . . D. Lamoureux

Fulfillment . . . . Casey M.

ANDREW THEITIC
Executive Editor

JEAN MARIE WALSH
Associate Editor

MAB BORDEN
Copy Editor

∾ Contents ∾

Contents

Est nemus et piceis et frondibus ilicis atrum.

    Vix illuc radiis solis adire licet.

Sunt in eo fuerant certe delubra Dianae:

    Aurea barbarica stat dea facta manu.

There is a wood, dark with spruce and boughs of oak;

the rays of the sun are scarcely even allowed to pierce it.

In that place, there is—or certainly there was—a sanctuary of Diana.

There stands the golden Goddess, fashioned by a barbarian hand.

Excerpt from *Heroides XII*
OVID

Yesterday, Today and Tomorrow

by Timi Chasen

PARDON ME It was hysteria that was the driving force behind the Witch hunts of the late Middle Ages. The frenzy swept through European society between 1450–1750. In many cases accusations were driven not only by wild fanaticism but also by greed, the property of the accused being ceased before they were even executed.

The hysteria swept with a particular fervence through Scotland, where the Witchcraft Act was instituted in 1563, being repealed in 1735. In the span of 172 years approximately 4,000 individuals were put to death, with the majority being women—in many cases they were widows or women over 40 years of age. In most cases the accused were hanged and then burnt at the stake.

Accusations of Witchcraft came from not only the disgruntled neighbor but also from the higher strata of society. The coastal town of North Berwick was at the center of the craze when King James VI accused the town's residents of using Witchcraft to thwart the arrival of his intended bride via ship from Denmark.

Marking 500 years since the passage of the Scottish Witchcraft Act, Scotland may be considering pardons for those that were put to death during the hysteria. On International Women's Day in 2020, a organization known as Witches of Scotland submitted a petition requesting the pardons to the government, with nearly 3,500 signatures. The leader of the Scottish National Party, First Minister Nicola Sturgeon, voiced support for the bill in late December 2021. This could lead to passage of a formal apology.

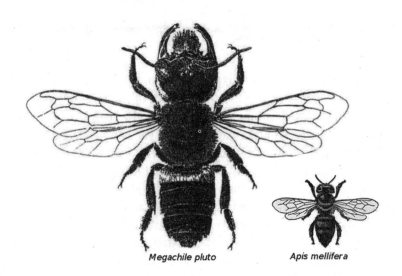

Megachile pluto   *Apis mellifera*

A LOT OF BUZZ The largest known bee is the *Megachile pluto*, that was first catalogued by the British naturalist Alfred Russel Wallace. This rather large member of the bee family is as large as an adult humans thumb and approximately four times the size of most bees. It has been known as "Wallace's giant bee" as well as the "giant mason bee."

It is native to the islands of Bacan, Halmahera and Tidore of Indonesia. Living a fragile existence in forests, it has been on the endangered species list for quite some time. Its natural habitat is being clear cut to make way for oil palm plantations.

These peculiar bees do not make nests of their own—instead they prefer to move into termite nests. They will segregate their habitation by building compartments that are walled with resin gathered from the now vulnerable species *Anisoptera thurifera*. Scientists believe that the relationship between the termites and the bees may be symbiotic.

Megachile pluto has been suspected extinct on a number of occasions. Prior to 1981 it was thought that the species had perished. Adam C. Messer, an American researcher, made the first documented encounter and study in 1981. He observed the bee collecting resin with its large mandibles. Post 1981 the bee was not further encountered until 2019 when Clay Bolt and Eli Wyman made the trip to Indonesia. Exhausted and ready to give up, they finally encountered a couple of nests, making observations and taking photos.

The biggest problem that faces these bees is the insatiable want of collectors. Several samples of *Megachile pluto* have shown up on Ebay.

AS ABOVE SO BELOW Off the west coast of Sicily once thrived a settlement of Phoenicians in their island city of Motya. Recent archaeological investigations have begun to yield some astonishing finds.

The Phoenician city dates from the eighth century BCE, being rediscovered by the archaeologist Joseph Whitaker in 1920s. The distinguishing feature of the site is the large artificial lake that initially was thought to be an extension of the harbor. Whitaker thought this to be a military installation.

Firmly believing this to site to be military in nature, archaeologist set about looking for typical structures associated with martial activities. They believed that the artificial lake was more than likely similar to the structures in Carthage. In fact, they could not have been further from the truth.

What the archaeologists had in fact encountered was one of the largest sacred pools in the ancient Mediterranean. Instead of finding military buildings they found a temple to the Phoenician God Ba'al—the god of fertility, known as Lord of the Earth as well as Lord of Dew and Rain.

Excavations in 2010 revealed that the lake in fact was not connected to the harbor and was a spring fed lake. It also came to light that this was a religious complex, not simply a temple and lake, with the lake being the central feature.

Once the entire complex revealed itself, the most interesting aspect of the site was discovered. The entire complex was aligned to the constellation of Orion. To the Phoenicians the constellation Orion was Ba'al in the night sky. The temple of Ba'al aligns with Orion at the Winter Solstice. It is also believed that the flat reflective surface of the lake served as a means of plotting the movements of the stars and planets.

THAT'S JUST BATTY There are very few creatures that have a taste for blood. Hematophagy, the scientific name for feeding on blood, is common in a number of insects, some fish and invertebrate worms, but is not at all common among mammals.

Looking at old Dracula films, it would be easy to see how some could believe that there are bats that feed off humans. Well, in the diverse family of bats there are just three species of vampire bats and none of them feed off human blood!

Looking at the evolutionary tree and traits of the three species of blood feeding bats (*Desmodus rotundus, Diphylla ecaudata and Diaemus youngi*) scientists believe that the mutation allowing for the change in diet occurred once. A common ancestor (being the subfamily *Desmodontinae*) seems to be indicated, with subsequent divergence taking place over time. Scientists have concluded that the subfamily *Desmodontinae* diverged from a subfamily of nectar and fruit eating bats.

While a strict diet of blood is high in proteins with some fats, it lacks energy-producing carbohydrates that mammals use to fuel their activities. It is genetic mutation that has allowed them to adapt their single food source to producing small amounts of metabolic energy. However, because of this deficit, vampire bats have to feed more frequently than their cousins in other bat families. Their social structure also provides that they will regurgitate a meal to share with others that were unsuccessful in the hunt. That being said, they seem to remember who shared food in the past and will repay those members of the group first.

www.TheWitchesAlmanac.com

Author Bios

Meet New Contributors

Mab Borden

Coby Michael

Fee

Johnathan Sousa

Josie Winter

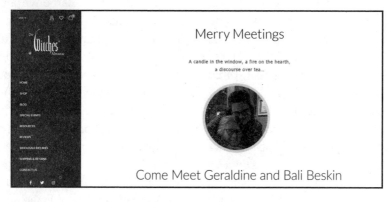

Merry Meetings

A candle in the window, a fire on the hearth,
a discourse over tea...

Come Meet Geraldine and Bali Beskin

Come visit us at the Witches' Almanac website

News from The Witches' Almanac

Glad tidings from the staff

It's been less than a year and we are hubbubing about in a crunch of time to put the final touches on *The Witches' Almanac* and get it out the door extra early. The weather in Rhode Island seems to be in as much of a tizzy as we are, running hot and cold for a fortnight! Just two weeks ago we were made aware that there are incredible backlogs at most printing presses. Our printer told us we needed to queue up in May to have the *Almanac* in September! We're Witches so instead of lamenting we got busy, we danced, sang, invoked, summoned and even stirred up the spirits and by the Gods we have delivered this on time. This is magic!

This year's big project was to improve the customer online shopping experience at TheWitchesAlmanac.com. We moved our store to the Shopify platform, while there were a few glitches—damn those gremlins—for the most part it was a smooth move. Our checkout process has been made seamless, there are more payment options and we have expanded our ship to locations. We have added wholesale ordering for small shops and business. A feature that we especially like is a new blog with the latest Almanac posts and it is even easier to signup for our newsletter.

This year's edition of *The Witches' Almanac* has many familiar faces as well as some new exciting authors. In Issue 42 we are joined by Mab Borden, Coby Michael, Fee, Johnathan Sousa and Josie Winter. Not to be missed this year is the *2023 Witches' Almanac Wall Calendar*. This year's theme is the Witches' herbs. As usual, there is rich imagery and a brief explanation of each herb.

In life people come into our lives and people journey out. This year we had to muster a goodbye to Ellen Lynch—of course there was a tear in our eyes and tightening in our throats. There are many who do their jobs well and Ellen did her job superlatively. She was not just a sales person, she was an advocate and a friend for many of our clients. Of course, with an equal amount of joy we welcome Roy Singleton in his role as our new sales person. Roy comes to us with over 30 years in customer service. He is here to make your Witches' Almanac experience a pleasant one!

The late Elizabeth Pepper designed *The Witches' Almanac's* logo after a very special sigil that she kept close to her heart. She had a small number of sterling silver pendants made in the 1980s, never making it available to the public. We have reproduced it, creating a sigil-pendant that can also be used as a charm—for a special bracelet or as a source of inspiration when doing private meditations or magical work. It can only be purchased at TheWitchesAlmanac.com.

We are in the third printing of *The 50 Year Anniversary Edition of The Witches' Almanac*, an anthology of articles published over the years. We knew you would love it!

SEEKING BALANCE

A new generation, technology and the Craft

IN THE CRAFT, one seeks to maintain a balance between experiencing what is here and what is Beyond. From observing the turning of the seasons to channeling the essence of the Gods, Witches make the whole range of actions their business. It is, however, not in the stereotypical repertoire of a Witch to be surfing on a mobile device for posts with metaphysical content. Conventionally, technology is seen as no means to that end, often rather a spiritual inhibitor to most. It is even more so this way now that in the digital age the internet seems to drag people by their imaginations into a sea of meaningless babble and gossip. There is still, however, great potential for the web to connect us in more enlightening ways which must not be overlooked. Social media is also a place for seekers and practitioners alike to bond over the occult. In this way it serves to link the lower worlds with the divine and the sacred. Most critically, certain apps are particularly effective at bridging generational gaps between old guard traditionalists and young users online who identify as Witches.

TikTok is the new name of a mobile app previously known as Musical.ly where people would lip sync over songs in short videos. Viewers can leave comments or cite clips in their own videos. From under a tag called cottagecore brewed an interest

❝

MUSICAL SCENES HAVE LONG BEEN A SAFE SPACE FOR PEOPLE TO FIND ACCEPTANCE AND THE OCCULT HAS BEEN NO EXCEPTION, ESPECIALLY SINCE THE 1960s.

in the folk-pagan aesthetic. Some posts under #cottagecore saw the opportunity to make posts romanticizing Witchcraft, and so WitchTok was born. There are three main archetypal critics of these posts known on the platform to pursue a few vastly different agendas. The first is the religious person who has always been there to call Witches Satanists and the like. By contrast, there are the skeptics who do not believe it is wrong but rather foolish to believe in the supernatural. The third subset includes learned magicians who constantly drive these influencers to higher standards of occult prestige.

While TikTok was becoming more popular, it was of course not the only haven for youth interested in these topics. Musical scenes have long been a safe space for people to find acceptance and the occult has been no exception, especially since the 1960s. But it is only recently that the underground rap scene at large has picked up a taste for Witchcraft. Another app called SoundCloud, which allows listeners to stream new music and comment on specific timestamps, is riddled with rappers dropping bars of marriage to the internet Witchcraft scene. Even popular artists of today are being associated with

Witchcraft unlike ever before. TikTok has been at the forefront of this dynamic every step of the way. WitchTok videos often include ethereal soundtracks over divinations or magical advice.

It is important to notice that in all this there is great potential for a huge new generation of initiates coming of age. This is not to say that these youth are statistically the most optimal candidates for the magical family, but that many of them are in fact disproportionately interested and will be knocking at elders' doors in droves in the future. It would be wise to periodically check on these societal progressions in social media by coordinating between coven members to stay up to date. To be the voice of the learned magician directly affects the quality of the conversation and works to spread accurate awareness about the craft to youth. Initiates have a unique ear for these conversations and will be able to distinguish between sophisticated and ignorant content. Coven leaders should know what to look for in the dispositions of young people. Through these means, elders can attract quality seekers in a more savvy way.

—FEE

The Legends of Sleeping Bear Dune and The Ghosts of Lake Nipissing

The Magic of the Manitou in Michigan and Ontario

MANITOU. The word means the mysterious cosmic power prevalent everywhere in nature. Manitou applies to the influences of a number of supernatural beings who dwell above, on and below the Earth. The word appears in different forms in a variety of Algonquin languages. Manitou is always applied to describe mystical events which strike deep and sincere chords of awe and wonderment.

The legend of Michigan's Sleeping Bear Dunes National Lakeshore is an especially intriguing and heartwarming story attributed to the intervention of Manitou. It is a traditional legend told by the Chippewa tribe. It began long ago with a fire in the forests of Northern Wisconsin, across Lake Michigan from the Northwest corner of the Lower Peninsula of Michigan. As the fire raged

a mother bear and her two cubs joined the other animals to flee from the smoke and flames. The family of bears were cornered on the shore. Their only choice was to plunge into the water and start swimming to safety. Mother bear led the way and kept looking back to encourage the cubs. At last the shoreline of Michigan came into sight, but the cubs fell behind. Mother bear climbed out of the water and turned to see her cubs coming into sight. She was tired and laid down to sleep until the little ones arrived. Sadly, they grew too tired to keep going and drowned just before reaching land. The Great Manitou Spirit intervened and turned the cubs into two islands near the beach. They came to be called North and South Manitou Islands. The mother bear was gently covered with sand by the Manitou and was turned into a bear-shaped dune. The family of bears sleeps blissfully, forever watched over by the kindly Manitou.

The outstanding beauty of this area led to its preservation as a National Wilderness by The United States Congress. In 2014 Sleeping Bear Dunes Park won a contest hosted by the television program Good Morning America, naming it as the most beautiful beach in the United States. The protected lakeshore is 35 miles long and encompasses both North and South Manitou Islands. Sleeping Bear Park is near Empire, Michigan and ferry service takes visitors to the islands.

Sleeping Bear Park offers unique flora and fauna, many historic and cultural points such as a lighthouse built in 1891, ghost towns abandoned by early settlers and prehistoric glacial phenomena. There is a historic village where you can explore more about the early days of life on the islands. Most of the entire area is available for hiking, camping and exploration. The 15,000 acres of North Manitou Island are managed as a wilderness area with the exception of the village. Manitou Island Transit provides regular ferry service to both islands for campers and day trips to South Manitou, which offers the only natural harbor along the Michigan shore for 200 miles.

Just Northeast of Michigan across the Great Lakes in Ontario, Canada, the mysterious influence of the Manitou spirit manifests in another wild place of great natural beauty. Ten kilometers—about 6 miles—southwest of North Bay, Ontario in Lake Nipissing is the Manitou Islands Provincial Park. This outstanding park is composed of 247 acres of land and five separate islands. First discovered in 1613 by Samuel de Champlain, they were praised for their beauty. Eventually fur traders passing through stopped there as a favorite camping spot. Lake Nipissing is the third largest lake within the Province of Ontario. The five islands are Great Manitou, Little Manitou, Calder, Newman and Rankin.

During the 1880s these islands developed in a flurry of activity. There was a lime quarry where a great kiln was built to make mortar for bricks, and Great Manitou once held a dance hall, hotel and other buildings. But the entire town burned to the ground. By the 1950s uranium was discovered and briefly mined on Newman Island. In 1972 the wreck of a steamship which had disappeared, the John B. Faber, was unexpectedly discovered in Lake Nipissing, between Goose Island and the Manitou Islands. The area has acquired the reputation of being haunted by a variety of spirits linked to a series of tragedies. These include the ghosts of the Nipissing, a tribe of Native Americans who faced starvation when forced from their island homes after losing battles with the Iroquois. Those who visit the Manitou Islands today report hearing the voices and seeing the spirits of those who once lived there and an eerie and quiet beauty marks the area.

The beautiful park has returned to a wilderness. Although there are no facilities nowadays, it can be reached easily by a passenger ferry or private boat. Hidden Gem Beach is a favorite destination for day trippers. The park is popular, but visitors seldom remain there for very long.

—ELAINE NEUMEIER

The Wild Hunt

GEESE HONKING overhead, the cawing of crows at night, dogs howling for no apparent reason—these are among the signals indicating that the Wild Hunt is passing above. Some people—especially Witches and the magically inclined—may also experience sensations of exhilaration, although others may feel an abrupt sense of dread or fear.

The Wild Hunt is the name given to a nocturnal procession of unruly, marauding spirits and ghosts. The head of the parade is known as the Wild Hunter, although there may be one leader or a pair. The parade itself is not orderly but raucous, *wild*. Witches are reputedly welcome to join in celebration, although the Wild Hunt also bears a reputation for terrorizing the sanctimonious and unwary.

The Wild Hunt manifests throughout the year, typically preferring the northern hemisphere's season of wild, stormy weather. Their appearances and presence are consistent and dependable enough that, when writing the recent book *Daily Magic: Spells and Rituals for Making the Whole World Magical*, a perpetual calendar, the Wild Hunt could be connected to specific dates and months. Although originating in Europe, the Wild Hunt has been witnessed in North America and elsewhere. Presumably, they go where they want.

Ghost riders in the sky

The concept of parades of spirits is not unique to the Wild Hunt nor is it exclusive to Europe. Other examples include cavalcading fairies, also known as trooping fairies, some of whose territory overlaps with that of the Wild Hunt. Unlike solitary fairies, these spirits also venture out in the form of processions. At Samhain the Wild Hunt and the trooping fairies are both out and about, although the fairies will likely retreat to their own realms afterwards, as they are not as fond of inclement weather as the Hunt.

Japan's Night Parade or the *Hyakki Yakō* consists of at least 100 spirits—assorted *yokai* and others—who march through Japan's streets at night, sometimes in an orderly fashion but sometimes as wild and chaotic as the Wild Hunt. Meanwhile, Hawaii's Night Marchers troop with military precision. Like the Wild Hunt, the Night Marchers are often accompanied by high winds, mist and thunderstorms. Some Gods such as Dionysus or Shiva are famed for leading entourages including ghosts in procession.

Wild Nights

The season of the Wild Hunt begins at Samhain (October 31st) or during the weeks leading up to it. The Wild Hunt is most perceptible when the veils between the worlds are sheer. Their season continues through the winter and typically ends with the start of Spring, although they may venture out on magically powerful nights such as Beltane. They are especially active between the Winter Solstice and Twelfth Night (January 5th or 6th.) Some believe Saint George's Day (April 23rd) marks the end of their season. In Central and Eastern Europe, Saint George's Day is considered a date of immense magical power, as described in Bram Stoker's novel, *Dracula*. The Wild Hunt plays a part in this dangerous ambience.

What may not be obvious to modern eyes is that the season of the Wild Hunt corresponds to the traditional pre-Christian European time of honoring the dead and welcoming ancestral ghosts back home. Many of the spirits associated with the Wild Hunt are shepherds of the dead and rulers of afterlife realms. It's believed that among their ancient roles, they supervised visitations by the dead to old haunts, as well as their return to their proper places in due time. This may have been the original role played by the Wild Hunt.

However, following mass European conversion to Christianity, perceptions of the Wild Hunt changed. Were they irrepressible spirits out to enjoy some revelry or were they hosts of Hell, doomed to ride restlessly as part of their punishment?

The Wild Hunt eventually became closely associated with Witchcraft. Those people who sought contact with them or even just wished to witness them were identified as Witches. The ghosts they led were no longer the beloved dead but were widely perceived as an army of the damned instead. Marching with the Hunt was perceived as punishment, not revelry; something that some dead souls were forced to do. The chief Wild Hunter was re-envisioned as a headhunter out collecting damned souls—those who had transgressed Christian laws and would now pay the price. People were warned that unbaptized babies were fated to join the Wild Hunt. Heathens, Jews, suicides and Witches were all widely believed doomed to wander endlessly with the Hunt.

or who ride alongside Odin as co-chief Hunters include Berchta, Freya, Herta and Hulda. Saint Lucy also sometimes rides beside Odin. However, some believe this Wild Hunt-riding aspect of Lucy is really Freya in disguise, the mask of the Christian saint providing a bit of syncretism that enables discreet veneration of the Pagan Goddess to survive, even if in secret.

The ghostly Matilda of the Night may also ride alongside Odin. According to legend, Matilda was a beautiful, irreverent Norman lady who loved hunting so much that she publicly announced that if there was no hunting in Heaven, she'd rather not go. Her wish was heard and Matilda's afterlife is spent leading bands of the Wild Hunt, sometimes accompanied by the hounds of Annwyn. The story of Matilda was intended as a cautionary tale: be an obedient Christian or spend eternity with the Wild Hunt. However, nothing indicates that she is unhappy.

Pandemonium

Odin is the star of the Wild Night, the primary Wild Hunter, although he has fierce competition from the Goddess Diana. If there is only one procession about and that procession only has one leader, it is likely to be one of them. They are not the only leaders of the Hunt, however, and sometimes competing processions ride out simultaneously. Other leaders include King Arthur; Arawn, Lord of Annwyn, a Welsh realm of death; the biblical Cain; Herne the Hunter; and Holler, the Norse winter king. When Arawn leads the Hunt, he is accompanied by his spectral hounds who bark and howl.

Herodias, a leading figure of Italian Witchcraft, may also lead the Hunt or she may ride alongside Diana. Northern Goddesses who frequently lead the Hunt

Safety tips

Avoidance is the best course of action for those who fear the Wild Hunt. If possible, stay inside on wild, windy, wintry nights. Should you encounter them accidentally, standard advice is to fall flat on the ground, make yourself as small and still as possible, and keep your eyes averted from them, essentially playing dead until you are sure they have completely passed. Stay calm, as various Wild Hunters find heightened emotions of any kind to be appealing. If avoiding them is impossible, reputedly politely requesting parsley provides safe passage. That kitchen herb has associations with the afterlife and is hallowed to various sacred beings. The word may be akin to a secret password or safe word that dissuades the Wild Hunt from causing harm.

Many, however, seek to revel with them and to experience the ecstasy of being in their presence. If that is your desire, folklore suggests that you are most likely to encounter the Wild Hunt at a crossroads. Choose a night they are likely to be about and congregate with Witches and kindred souls. Celebrate, throw a party if you can—the Hunt enjoys high spirits and heightened, excited emotions. Dance or twirl outside in the wind, assuming that it's safe to do so. Shut your eyes and see if you can *feel* the Wild Hunt. Those with second sight or heightened extra-sensory perceptions may be able to view or hear them.

Gifts of the season

The Wild Hunt sometimes distributes gifts. If you are at a crossroads after dark and the Wild Hunt arrives, rumor has it that if you stand calmly and quietly as the Wild Hunt rides by, the final Hunter will distribute coins. These are spectral coins—lucky amulets—rather than actual coinage. Do not spend the coin or give it away but preserve it as a charm—a money magnet—that allegedly attracts more money and will help you accrue a fortune. A competing legend suggests that should you receive such a coin, you will be unable to part from it. No matter how many times you spend it, lose it or give it away, that coin will always return to you. This ritual is believed especially efficacious on Christmas Eve, but it may be attempted at any time. Fasting during daytime hours before you encounter the Hunt is believed to help.

Reputedly, the Wild Hunters are especially likely to distribute gifts on Christmas Eve. This may be understood as a very subversive legend, vestigial European resistance to Christianity: spend Christmas Eve reveling with the Hunt rather than praying in Church and receive gifts, not damnation.

—JUDIKA ILLES

BONE INSTRUMENTS

Animism, Atavism and Agency

Behold, I will cause breath to enter into you, and ye shall live.

Ezekiel 37:5

THE USE OF BONES within musical performance practice spans millennia. Far from being solely associated with macabre and necromantic associations—although in some cases and cultures this is clearly evident—bone is an available material which additionally affords the magical practitioner opportunities to connect in a physical manner with the animal or indeed person the bone came from.

While this essay focuses primarily upon bone aerophones—instruments which make sound through vibrating a mass of air—there are many examples to be found of bone instruments amongst all of the categories of instruments. There are described by Hornbostel-Sachs as bone chordophones (instruments which produce sound through the vibration of a string stretched between two fixed points), bone idiophones (instruments which produce sound through the body of the instrument vibrating) and bone membranophones (instruments which produce sound through the vibration of a stretched membrane.) That the membrane used in the creation of membranophones may also be made of skin is also of interest, but outside the remit of this article.

Some of the earliest extant instruments are flutes made from bones or bone-like materials. In particular, early surviving bone flutes are often discovered to have been constructed from bird bone or ivory. A recent discovery in 2008 of an ice age flute made from a griffon vulture wing bone in Hohle Fels, Germany has enabled researchers to recreate the instrument and

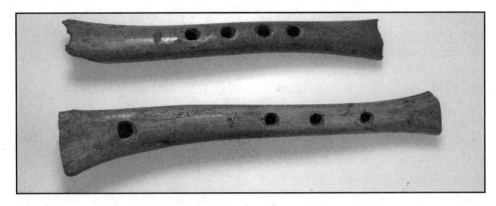

discover how it may have sounded. It is currently believed that the narrow nature of the bone would produce pitches in a manner similar to the more recent Tabor pipe which is popular in the Pyrenees, Iberian Peninsula and the Balearic Islands. A 3D view of the flute can be found on the website of the Urgeschichtliches Museum in Blaubeuren, Germany and audio of the reconstructed flutes may be heard at the museum.

Similar bone flutes from this period (35,000–40,000 BCE) include those made of swan bone, ivory and—more specifically—mammoth ivory. The mammoth ivory flute is noted as being "surprisingly loud" and produces eight tones. The technicality of its construction is unparalleled amongst Paleolithic instruments but we cannot know with any certainty if its intended use held any ritualistic or animistic significance.

There are later examples of bone flutes from the Anglo-Saxon and medieval periods with hundreds of examples being found across England illustrating the prominence of this instrument at the time. Here again many of the flutes are made from bird wing bones (predominantly geese)

or the tibia of mammals (mainly sheep). It is believed that a proportion of the sheep tibia flutes have been misidentified and are in fact made from deer metatarsal. These deer flutes have been found near larger towns, often associated with castles and as such there have been examples found at Winchester and Keynsham Abbey near Bath in England. This supports the understanding of deer hunting practices undertaken by the upper classes of society at that time.

These animal bone flutes are rudimentary in design, especially those of bird bone which often have only three finger holes. They may be crafted by using a knife. It would therefore be possible for a person to create a flute for ritual purposes from the bone of an animal whose magical correspondences would be beneficial to their ritual. Examples of such values may be seen below.

Animal	Magical Association
Swan	The soul, grace
Deer	Strength, independence
Eagle	Renewal, intelligence
Kite	Freedom, joy

Until recently the Divje Babe flute—a flute constructed from the femur of a cave bear—was thought to be the oldest surviving instrument at almost 44,000 years old. The flute was discovered in 1995 in the Northwest of Slovenia and is on public display in the National Museum of Slovenia. However, recent research by paleoanthropologists has suggested that its holes, rather than being the work of a somewhat artisanal Neanderthal were in fact made by the teeth of other animals, most likely Ice Age hyenas.

There is, however, a tradition within Tibetan Buddhism of ceremonial musical instruments, in particular aerophones, being made out of bones such as the femur or tibia. These instruments, called *kangling* which literally translates as leg-flute, have been used since the 17th century within Chöd rituals, often to symbolise the lack of fear within the practitioner or to summon spirits deemed to be hungry who may then be fed, thus alleviating their suffering. For the construction of a kangling, the leg bone of someone who died a violent death or that of a criminal is preferable. The kangling should be played alongside the chöd damaru, a membranophone whose skin is buried for several weeks and whose purpose is to act as a channel for the energies of one's ancestors, both familiar and spiritual. The bell which is also included in the performance is cast from bronze and held in the left hand while the chöd damaru is held in the right.

Leg flutes and bone flutes have a history of use within some Traditional

Witchcraft lineages. This praxis continues today where the instrument serves the purpose of summoning or banishing Spirit within ritual or as a signal to those present that portions of the ritual are due to commence. The symbolism of the instrument in such cases can be seen as a physical representation of the concept of Witch Blood and the acknowledgement and incorporation of atavistic power or knowledge within the ritual and one's own workings.

The quijada de burro is an Afro-Peruvian idiophone which is made from the jawbone of a donkey, horse or mule. The unique buzzing sound of the instrument is produced by holding the jawbone at the narrow end and hitting the larger end of the jawbone with the hand or a stick, causing any remaining teeth in the jawbone to rattle. It is believed that the instrument was first used by enslaved people during the colonial era and its popularity is still evident in Peru today and also among Latin American cultures across Argentina, Mexico and the Dominican Republic where it forms a central role within folk music performance.

Although it is not a bone, Ivory is one the most well known animal materials used in instrument making over the centuries. An olifant is the name given to a hunting horn made from an elephant and these were popular amongst the wealthy during the Middle Ages. Examples of these horns exist to this day, one such example being the Oliphant of Ulph,

dated to the early eleventh century and now held within the treasure of York Minster in the cathedral of York, England. The eleventh century epic poem *La Chanson de Roland* (The song of Roland) includes Roland's use of his olifant to attempt to summon Charlemagne's army. This emphasizes the volume of the instrument which enables it to be heard from a great distance and again points towards the role of bone aerophones within summoning or dismissing.

When practitioners combine their breath with the bone of another being with the sole purpose of creating a sound, they bring that bone back to life to a greater or lesser degree. Bone instruments used as a tool for magical praxis should therefore be revered as fetishes of the beings they were in life. With this understanding bone instruments may be advanced beyond the usual understanding of working tools, becoming valuable allies to the Witch.

—JERA

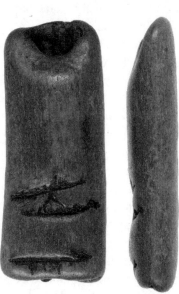  

Albrecht Dürer (1471-1528)

Dazzling then, dazzling now

Dürer's self portrait at 26

READERS of the Almanac may be familiar with the superb drawings of Dürer, for his graphics have turned up often within these pages. He was the favorite illustrator of our late publisher Elizabeth Pepper, herself an artist and sometime engraver. Dürer towers over the history of printmaking as Shakespeare towers over poetry, clearly its master. The artist's work expresses soaring vision and drafting technique unequaled before or since, reflecting religion, mythology, folklore and history.

A painter and art theorist as well as printmaker, absorbed in philosophy and science, Dürer was a true Renaissance man.

Dürer was born in Nuremberg, Germany, his father a prosperous goldsmith from Hungary. The family had from fourteen to eighteen children, either way a daunting family. At the age of fifteen Dürer apprenticed to Michael Wolgemut, joining a shop that produced diverse work, including books illustrated with woodcuts. Young Dürer was in the right place at the right time. With the advent of printmaking, for the first time artists had no need of royal patrons and ordinary people could have prints in their homes. While Dürer created an exquisite body of paintings, he turned more and more to prints in later life, declaring that woodcuts, engravings and silverpoints were more profitable. By the time Dürer was twenty he had become famous, both in Germany and in Italy.

In addition to his extensive body of artwork, Dürer wrote and produced two books still available: *Fortification* and *The Painter's Manual: Instructions on Measurement*, largely dealing with geometry and perspective. Most of the artist's paintings are in private collections, but his former home in Nuremberg has become a Dürer museum. More than five centuries later the architectural A.D. initials on a print always confirm a unique genius—for example the opposite page: "The Knight, Death and the Devil," 1513, enigmatic and gloriously crafted, a masterpiece of copperplate engraving.

The Knight, Death and the Devil
Albrecht Durer (1471-1528)

Deadly Nightshade

The Witch's Swiss Army Knife

IF YOU COULD only choose one herb to work with for the rest of your magical life, what would it be? You could ask any magical practitioner that works with herbs this question and probably get multiple answers from each one. When considering which plant to work with as a spirit ally, there is always one plant that comes to mind immediately. Magical work infuses its very essence—perhaps this is just the form that a familiar spirit has decided to take. The plant is *Atropa belladonna* or deadly nightshade.

The plants of the Poison Path fall under the rulership of Saturn as their corresponding planet. Saturn—known as the greater malefic in astrology—is the first indicator of these plants' baneful natures. A baneful herb is anything that has a connection to what humans consider dark, dangerous or untamable. Baneful herbs don't have to be poisonous, as there are many other ways that nature can act as an adversary to humans. Not all Saturnian herbs are poisonous but all poisonous herbs fall under Saturn's reign.

Poison is a warning label. It tells you not to get too close. However, this is the purpose of the Poison Path—to explore all the subtleties of balm and bane. Armed with an inquisitive mind, daring spirit and at least a small sense of self-preservation, you can approach these entities that are so different from humans with a level of respect. Poisonous plants do not care whether you live or die, just as medicinal plants have no personal stake in your recovery or healing. This is the relationship through the lens of your human experience. There are many ways to connect with these master plant spirits and incorporate them into your magic that do not require you to put yourself at risk.

The Devil's favorite plant

By looking at belladonna you will see some of the potential for working with plants on the Poison Path that do not require self in-TOXIC-ation. Belladonna always holds a certain allure as many first hear about it in the film Practical Magic. In occult explorations, however, you will discover the powerful potential of this plant and those like it. Belladonna or deadly nightshade is a member of the Nightshade family, often referred to as Witching or hexing herbs because of their poisonous and psychoactive potential and their ancient association with Witchcraft. Many plants in this family have an extensive history in both medicinal and ceremonial uses, including plants like henbane, datura and the infamous mandrake.

Belladonna is set apart from many others in that it doesn't have much in the way of surviving magical or ceremonial uses. This is not to say that the plant wasn't ever used ceremonially, but that people likely opted for less dangerous options. It is called deadly nightshade for a reason. The margin of error for other nightshades is a little wider, but this is less so with belladonna. It sneaks up on you, luring you in with a false sense of security, catching you in a web of sinister and terrifying visions.

Deadly nightshade was definitely present in the folklore of medieval Europe. It was demonized for its baneful nature by Hildegard von Bingen in the 12th century. By looking at the common names for the plant you can gain a glimpse of its place in medieval folklore. On the surface belladonna's name means "beautiful lady" in Italian. However, further investigation reveals her more sinister nature. It is often referred to by names that translate to Witch's berry or Witch's plant and the same is true for its epithets that refer to the devil. It is also called wolf's berry which associates it with Odin and Wotan, as well as Valkyrie berry. It's scientific name Atropa belladonna comes from the Greek Atropos, the inexorable Fate responsible for cutting the thread of life. It is also associated with the Greek Furies. Other names refer to its deadly, intoxicating and sleep-inducing effects. One thing is for certain, that belladonna is a plant of the spirit world, marked by otherness and connected to the chthonic forces of death, chaos and fate. It is no wonder that deadly nightshade was known as the Devil's favorite plant. The prescribed method for harvesting the Devil's coveted plant was to approach it

passions and to change perception, like many Witches! Belladonna and plants like it are magical catalysts. They have such an extensive and intimate affinity with the spirit world that they become potent allies in magical practice beyond their uses as ingredients based on correspondence. They bring their own unique power and agency to a ritual— not to say other plants don't, but magical catalysts have an extra willingness to work with the occult practitioner.

Belladonna in practice

The spirit of belladonna is often described as a dark and beautiful woman and there is a definite element of seduction and sexuality about this plant. Its uses as a Renaissance cosmetic preparation and aphrodisiac make belladonna a potent component in workings related to love, lust and sex. It can be worked with as an herb of influence and persuasion, being both beguiling and dominating in its approach. Including belladonna berries or flowers in related formulas for their tempting appeal, the plant can be incorporated into oils, ritual baths and incense when used sparingly.

Belladonna is also attributed with Mars-like qualities because of an ancient connection to the Roman War Goddess Bellona. Capable of inducing madness and frenzy, belladonna unleashes her unpredictable force on the battlefield. A powerful herb of protection, deadly nightshade has both Saturnian and Martial qualities useful for offensive as well as defensive magic, and that are both powerful and long lasting. The herb has won its share of battles and was used as an ancient bioweapon. The Scottish King Duncan I won a battle by poisoning an

on Walpurgisnacht, the one night of the year the plant was left unattended.

The plant was often approached as a means of contacting the spirit world and the unseen forces that remain hidden in the darkness. It can be thought of as a kind of a gateway or a place where the veil is thin due to the plant's baneful nature. At the base of the plant and in its branches offerings were left in payment for requests made to the Old One. It was a plant approached with caution because it was believed to be inhabited by spirits, Witches and the Devil himself.

Belladonna has much magical potential as a component of spell craft and also as a tutelary spirit. It is one of the quintessential Witching herbs, representing the traditional medieval Witch archetype. Belladonna is simultaneously poisonous, aphrodisiacal, medicinal and psychoactive. It has the power to heal, to harm, to raise entire army with the Valkyries' berry. Deadly nightshade will potentiate any protection formula when added. The seeds can be crushed and added to protection powder to lay boundaries around the home and the roots can be worked into fetishes that can be placed around the home to act as wards.

As one of the quintessential Witching herbs, belladonna is capable of all the things accused of medieval Witches, including spirit flight, hexing, raising storms and all forms of maleficia. The berries are perfect to use as the hearts of poppets meant for workings of a dark nature. The herb has the ability to both summon and banish spirits, as is the case with many herbs of ceremonial significance. It was used by the Sumerians in cases of demonic possession. Deadly nightshade was one of the commonly cited ingredients in the medieval Witches' flying ointments and was known throughout history for its trance inducing effects.

With its entheogenic potential, belladonna can be used as a plant spirit ally in rituals relating to the Witches' Sabbath, nocturnal flight and spirit communication. It is of especial significance at Samhain and Beltane. An herb of shamanic travel, belladonna specifically grants access to the Underworld or chthonic realms where the ancestors, nature spirits and other terrestrial spirits reside.

It is a divinatory herb, best used during the dark Moon. Scrying, necromancy and dream incubation are all enhanced by the energy of deadly nightshade, which can be accessed through the use of anointing oils, flower essences and flying ointments. It is known for the effect it has on the pineal gland, the part of the brain that regulates psychic senses, dreams and the sleep cycle. Whether working with the plant vibrationally or applying it topically, belladonna has profound effects on the subtle senses and is an excellent herb for divination. It can be used to connect with the primal power of the Fates themselves or to tap in to the fate of a specific situation for insight.

Plant spirit familiar

Working with a plant spirit is very much the same as working with any other familiar spirit. There is a regular exchange of energy and information between the Witch and the familiar. Offerings are made and regular medita-

Belladonna Plant Spirit Glyph

tion and ritual is performed to interact with the plant spirit, which will often come to the Witch in visions, dreams and insights. Many will often choose to grow the plant associated with their familiar to connect with it on both a physical and spiritual level. For some practitioners, this is the extent of their work with plant spirit familiars. Others will work with their plant by ingesting small amounts in ways that are safe and appropriate for that specific plant or will work with it in a vibrational way.

The relationship between the practitioner and the plant spirit is typically long term and develops over time. The plant spirit often acts as an intermediary, connecting the Witch to other spirits. Oftentimes specific agreements or pacts between the practitioner and the plant spirit are made and these are typically unique to the individual. Such an agreement might include something like adhering to a diet which combines fasting and consuming only specific plant materials or honoring a set of predetermined taboos. These ordeals are meant to confer personal power and knowledge when they are maintained.

Being associated with the folkloric Devil, belladonna is a perfect candidate whether you wish to work with plant spirits or otherwise. It can be used in rituals to seal pacts and make them binding. Just the presence of the living plant or its dry plant material is enough to connect to the powerful spirit that resides in the shadow of this plant's leaves. You can incorporate *Atropa belladonna* in ritual and spell work in virtually all of the same ways that you would any other magical plant. Create strong infused oils from the dry plant material for both medicinal and magical purposes or use it as an ingredient in other formulas for spell work. Small amounts can be used in incense formulas and it can be incorporated into charm bags and ritual jewelry of all sorts. Much like its cousin mandrake, the talismanic power of this plant is undeniable and simply carrying small amounts with you is enough to bring its effects into your life. Poison rings, tiny bottles and charm bags are all safe ways to keep your plant spirit ally nearby, which is necessary for forging a deep connection.

The main thing to remember when working with poisonous plant allies is the diversity of ways that a plant can be worked within a spiritual capacity. This doesn't mean that you have to go around eating all of the plants that you want to work with or that you have to ingest them to alter your consciousness. There are very effective ways of working with these spirits sympathetically that do not require putting yourself at risk. With that being said, poisonous does not equate to radioactive and these plants should be approached with love and understanding like all of the Earth's creatures. Remember knowledge over fear—this is the alchemical formula that transmutes poison into magic and magic into medicine. However, there is a level of assumed risk when you decide to work with plants on the Poison Path and everyone must be held accountable for their own decisions and interactions that involve these plants. By choosing to step onto the Poison Path, you are making a conscious decision and doing so at your own risk.

—COBY MICHAEL

THE BUSINESS OF WITCHCRAFT

ONE OF THE KEY lessons to learn from Witchcraft is that there's always an exchange of energy involved. Time and effort spent is a kind of currency, whether you're meditating, performing rituals, making offerings, crafting spells, gathering wisdom or tending to people, places and things.

Yet quite a few Witches tend to get uneasy when you mention business and money in reference to Witchery. The phrases "you shouldn't make money from the Craft" or "you shouldn't use magic for personal gain" might pop up. However, it's worth noting that the sources for these sayings stem out of a mixture of fiction, fantasy and financial privilege more than practical wisdom. Not only are these ideas quite modern in

origin but they are very narrow ways of looking at both history and practice—as well as money. We don't ask our farmers, lawyers or doctors to give away their services or expertise. We understand that donating to a church or temple helps keep it running and we pay taxes to fund education. Meanwhile magic has a long history of being used precisely to better one's own world or community. It's long been a tool of the marginalized and disenfranchised to bring about change and gain power. We need to be able to view Witchcraft within the same reality to honor our practice.

Witch business is small business.
In the modern-day magical community, those who use the term Witch tend to do so in religious or spiritual terms or as

an identity. Whether one believes there are ties to ancient religions found within contemporary Witchcraft or it's something newly conjured in the last century, what is clear is that many of the things we consider part of a Witchcraft practice fell historically under the heading of a vocation. Cunningfolk, healers, herbalists, mediums, diviners and midwives all provided services for their communities—it's how they made a living—just like bakers, farmers, blacksmiths, etc.

Whether you write esoteric books, make magical art or music, craft oils and teas, make candles, create jewelry, offer readings, teach classes, run a store, provide healing service or throw events, etc.—*or are the customer for any of these things*—there's an exchange to be considered. Money (be it cash or credit) is what we use most often in modern society to validate the exchange. That money stands in for the transfer of energy that can no longer be conducted by offering five chickens or six bags of wheat. That's not to say barter or trade doesn't happen nowadays, but it's a lot harder to pay for gas or the electric bill with physical goods or services. So we use money instead, a symbol for that trade. It's also a little more easy to fit into your wallet!

That's not to say mixing money with Witchcraft can't be problematic, but it's better to understand the how and why in order to have a healthy understanding. There's been a tendency to conflate commerce with capitalism so it's important to recognize that we're talking about paying people fairly for their time, expertise, services and goods—whether that's via money, work exchange, trade or other kinds of barter.

Merging secular & spiritual

Being spiritual doesn't excuse the realities of being alive. Most societies take care of their clergy. These clergy typically receive housing, food and a respectable stipend for their time and service. While some paths have a vow of poverty, those who practice these paths typically still have their basic needs taken care of by the larger organization, community donations or selling some sort of product to cover costs. Many kinds of churches and temples raise money through their services and products.

While there are now numerous federally recognized Pagan temples, churches and non-profits, most practitioners are independent or part of small groups. That means that they are responsible for taking care of their own needs vs. having them provided by their society. Therefore they are more likely to charge for their services to pay the bills.

That said, you DON'T have to make money off of your practice! You can be a Witch and have a mundane job. You don't have to write a book, sell candles, do readings, run a shop, etc. to be a Witch. Nor does it have to be a spiritual calling for you. Every Witch's path is different.

Keeping the broom clean

Here are some things to consider in order to have a healthier relationship with money and Witchcraft:

- Value yourself, value your work. You can make a gift of what you do but don't de-value your work—or that of others—in the process.
- You get what you pay for—or don't. It's an unfortunate truth that people value things they pay for more than those they obtain for free or little effort.
- Learn to say no, especially when it comes to clients and customers. Keep healthy boundaries and communicate as clearly as possible what the terms and conditions are.
- Focus on quality, not quantity. You'll find that your time tends to be more wisely invested in that which you spend more time on, be it an art, craft or education.
- Find your own niche and be true to yourself—avoid copying or stealing from others. Trends come and go but originality lasts.
- Exercise transparency when it comes to finances with groups, events and other activities. This means explaining costs and expenses, doing proper accounting and taking care of the necessary paperwork .

- Everyone should feel valued for their contribution even if they wish to donate their time. If there's a trade or apprenticeship situation, all parties should understand what is expected from everyone involved.
- Keep in touch with the needs of the community you work in so that you have a handle on the local news, economics and social developments. Invest in what you believe in.

The world doesn't make it easy to be a practicing Witch as it is, let alone to be one who is out in the public charging for services. Plenty of laws have been enacted to prevent or curb fraudulent mediumship, predatory divination and dangerous products (i.e., snake-oil salesmanship.) For the last couple of decades many practitioners have run into difficulties with credit card processors who refuse to have anything to do with you if your product or service includes words such as "psychic," "spell," or "magic." At the same time, plenty of "normal" businesses swindle folks every day in plain sight—just ask the BBB! Our challenge is to practice fairly, openly, valuing ourselves, our services and each other.

—LAURA TEMPEST ZAKROFF

In the Depths

The primordial energies of Earth

THERE IS ONLY so far down you can go before Earth no longer wishes to give up her secrets. Water wells can typically be dug by hand, with the deepest water well—the Woodingdean Well in Brighton and Hove in England—plunging 1,280 feet. Most are much more shallow and many are driven or bored. The deepest wells in the world are drilled, though, and at such great depth that Earth no longer provides humankind with life-sustaining water, but with oil—toxic and potent.

The Moon card in the tarot suggests that what crawls out of the deep subconscious might not be as lovely as the querent might like, the clattering crawfish being a critter of nightmare more frequently than of daydream, culinary fancy notwithstanding. Likewise with Earth. The upper areas of Earth contain caves of spiritual mystery and inspiration as well as material wealth, and the wells at this level are those of Mimir—requiring sacrifice but granting much more than is given. The seeker who would plumb the depths should be prepared for something less appealing and far more powerful. The spiritual experience of the deep wells of Earth is no lighter than their physical reality—as above, so below.

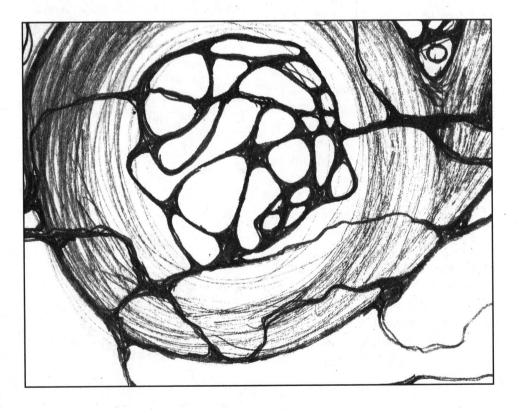

Before it seeps out of the deep Earth, oil seeps from bones. The primordial yellow-black ooze that is petroleum in its crude state is the recycled goo from the cauldron of corpses. It holds the life of multitudes of ancient creatures, many extinct. Crude oil is formed from their remains, pressed under layers of rock so heavy and so hot that they combine, liquify and transform. How the power of this multitude is employed can both save and destroy life, but its impact is always immense.

Anyone who has smelled an oil rig from miles away knows how sharp, ugly and undeniable that power is, and it cannot be mistaken for a place of pilgrimage. Why seek the spiritual sustenance of this layer of Earth, then? Is it not simply one of the monsters that Gaia birthed in the tales of the Greeks? If so, then what shall you do with monsters? This one is already filling up the ocean with bottles and burning holes in the ozone layer, and simultaneously making intubation and dialysis possible, but what will you do with it? That answer is for the individual to consider before diving deeper than the groundwater.

Wells of all kinds serve to gather in the resources of Earth that soak her bones, but how can you withstand the overpowering and poisonous nature of this particular psychic resource? Look again to the physical aspect of this form of Earth. The deepest well in the world is the Chayvo oil field in Russia, at 3,300 feet deep—nearly three times the depth of the Woodingdean Well. The oil well's length, though, is 49,000 feet as it moves horizontally and diagonally as

well as vertically. The spiritual seeker of Earth's depths should move likewise. Drilling might seem like a very yang sort of activity, a forceful driving of one's will into the object of power. But the physical winding of the deepest wells suggests a dance between Earth and the one who would court her for the substance of her strength.

The deepest gold mine in the world—in Mponeng, South Africa—is nearly ten thousand feet deeper than the oil wells of the Chayvo field, hinting that perhaps what you have to work harder to chip from the stone is more precious and more true than what passively seeps.

—MAB BORDEN

Hoodoo—Conjuration—Witchcraft—Rootwork

an excerpt regarding spirits and ghosts

Harry Middleton Hyatt's masterwork, *Hoodoo—Conjuration—Witchcraft—Rootwork*, which he self-published in five thick volumes during the years 1970–1978, has long been almost impossible to obtain. The Witches' Almanac hopes to remedy this unfortunate situation, having published all five volumes in 2020.

[The belief in spirits is the foundation of hoodoo, conjuration, witchcraft, rootwork and similar superstitions. Everywhere throughout this investigation spirits are mentioned or assumed.]

One Spirit

22. [Despite the preceding title *Two Spirits*, they are two in character but one in substance.]

I have hear'n people say that your spirit travels—it is out walking around at places where you have worked. You're sleeping and maybe you're trying to wake up—you're having a hard time waking. If you die, your spirit is gone from you, they say. It takes a long time to get it back. Some people are hollering and hollering and can't move. You're supposed to go and put your hand on them and shake them till they speak to you. They say you sometimes dies in that condition. People say they have hear'n this, people making a noise through the night. They think they were dreaming and they didn't bother, pay any attention to them. Next morning the're late getting up.

When they go to rouse them, they would be dead. [New York, (6), Ed.]

23. If that spirit goes out somewhere and gets killed or drownded, it·will not return and the body lays dead. [Old Point Comfort, (24), Ed.]

Part of Spirit Equals Whole of Spirit

24. [There used to be a mathematical axiom stating that *the whole is the sum of all its parts.* In hoodoo, however, a part can equal the whole. Every part and function of your body (hair and breath)—anything touching you (clothes and bathwater)—whatever signifies you (name and photograph)—all these and others are substitutes for either the whole or part of ·the spirit. Many examples of this belief will be found elsewhere—here are a few:]

25. Yo' could· write a person name on a piece of papah an' throw it ovahbo'd an' it would cause dem to go. It would cause dem to jump ovahbo'd—jes' like yo' throw it in a rivah, it would cause dem to go an' jump in de rivah. [Brunswick, Ga., (1175), 1987:6.]

26. Get a little box—a tin box. Put dat toenails in there and fingernails in there, cayenne pepper, *war water*—you get the *war water, devil dust.* You puts in there and you stop that can up tight, you see, and bury it. Den when you bury it, the person what it belongs to, their hand'll come like that - they'll draw up.

(Draw up - drawn up.)

Yeah, all drawn up. If it stay longer, the more it draw. They won't be no use for theirself.

(What is *devil dust?*)

Devil dust is what you get in the [hoodoo] drug store. [New Orleans, .La., (798), 1113:5.]

27. Take your handwritin'—see, de handwritin' where it was writ wit ink or lead. Dey take it and soak it in water and get dat ink, get dat ink off it from your handwritin'. Den dey will take dat water and boil it. See. Den take dat water and

pour it out gradualy—don't pour dat all at one time, jes' kinda sprinkle it along. When dat water pour out chew begin tuh feel bad—yo' hand begin to feel nervous up thru yo' arms and finally, if you don't know what to do, yo' become paralyzed in your right hand. [Washington, D. C., (638), 824:2.]

28. A man, he tole me his ole lady went outdoors one night an' went to her chicken coop an' got a big sack fulla chicken dirt—taken it in de house an' taken ashes out de fireplace an' taken his underwears an' rolled dis stuff up in it an' taken—yo' know, rolled it ovah. Didn't mess wit it any way atall—jes' rolled it ovah an' take it out an' carried it to his bed an' washed his feet, an' let de watah drene off his feet into that ashes an' chicken stuff, an' says, he can't even walk now. Says, lak if he walks, seems lak needles stickin' in him.

(Was he asleep—she did that while he was asleep?)

No, he wusn't asleep—he jes' thought she wus washin' his feet. Dat's all, but he had noticed dat. [Fayetteville, N. Car., (1403), 2526:4.]

29. Dey tell me dat dey kin take yore bath water and bury it. Dig a hole and pore it in dere and put a piece of - jest a small piece of bluestone, sulphur an' asafitadee [assafetida] in dat hole with dat water and cover it up. And dey tell me dat will keep yo' perishing away all de time. [Mobile, Ala., (701), 951:9.-]

Hoodoo—Conjuration—Witchcraft—Rootwork is available at https://TheWitchesAlmanac.com/collections/new-releases/products/works-on-hoodoo-and-folklore-harry-m-hyatt

Los Antepasados

An Excerpt From J. Allen Cross'
American Brujeria

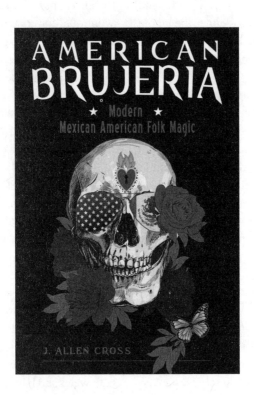

ONE OF MY MAIN goals for this book is to connect people to their ancestors by bringing back the traditions and magic of our people. So what better way to connect with our ancestors than through veneration and working with them in our daily spiritual practices? We as Mexican American people know that they never truly leave us, and death is a celebrated part of our culture. In this chapter we will cover the basics of working with our beloved dead and how we can incorporate them into our daily lives once more.

Building an Ancestor Altar

Building an ancestor altar is very simple and doesn't have to take up much space. Much like when we make a saint altar, we want to be sure that the area is clean both physically and spiritually. After that, though, the construction is largely up to you, so feel free to be creative! Some common things that are placed on the altar are photos of the deceased; items that belonged to them such as rosaries, Bibles, or jewelry; things that they enjoyed in life like favorite cigarettes, favorite liquor, or favorite perfume; as well as items for spiritual maintenance such as holy water or Florida Water. These last two can be used to clean and bless the altar as necessary. I also like to have a Bible near, if not on, the altar so that I can perform bibliomancy when asking for guidance.

The other things you'll want on the altar are a white candle, a glass of water, and incense. These are used in much the same way as we've described in previous chapters. The candle acts as a beacon for your ancestors. The water is an offering and a conduit their energy. The incense helps elevate them and carries our prayers up to heaven. These things together allow us to facilitate the connection between ourselves and their spirits. In order to maintain a strong connection, be sure to keep your altar clean both physically and energetically so it remains a pure conduit for their spirits. Dirty altars are not pleasant for them to inhabit, and they're likely to leave. They also attract negative spirits that may try to harm us.

Taboos

Certain things are considered taboo or forbidden when it comes to the ancestor altar, and they are important to discuss. The first is that photos of the living should not be placed on the ancestor altar. This is said to bring the living person a speedy death.

The second most common taboo is placing ancestor altars in the bedroom. Our bedroom is where we often get naked and engage in sexual activities that the family does not really want to watch. Plus, many folks who have loud or intrusive families find it difficult to sleep when their ancestors are in their room at night. This issue can be complicated because sometimes we don't have room anywhere else or we live in a studio apartment where our bedroom is our whole house. What do we do then? First, you may wish to cover your ancestor altar with a sheet at night before you go to bed or before any nudity or sexual activities. You may also put up a partition screen or a room divider to create a separate space between the ancestors and the rest of the room.

Some folks also say that you should not let salt anywhere near your ancestor altar as it chases away the dead. They often go so far as to say that any food you offer them should not contain any salt. I don't feel this way about the food: the ancestors deserve flavor. Also, we need to remember that a popular *Día de los Muertos* tradition says to put a dish of salt on the *ofrenda* (offering) to keep bad spirits at bay. I think where people get confused is that earthbound spirits (those who haven't crossed over) can be troublesome and are repelled by earthly things like salt. However, the ancestors that we are working with have crossed over and are no longer susceptible to such trivial things. Others also say that burning cleansing herbs will chase them away, but I've also found this to be a myth for

Some common things that are placed on the altar are photos of the deceased; items that belonged to them such as rosaries, Bibles, or jewelry; things that they enjoyed in life like favorite cigarettes, favorite liquor, or favorite perfume; as well as items for spiritual maintenance such as holy water or Florida Water.

the same reasons. In fact, I always burn cleansing herbs before calling them forth as I find it helps them come through more clearly with less interference.

Working with the Ancestors

Once your altar is set up, you may begin working with the ancestors. If you are the first in your family to do this, they may be a little sleepy or in need of maintenance. Either way, be sure to spend some time lighting novenas, feeding them, and saying prayers before you begin to ask for favors. This introductory period should last at least a month, after which you may begin to make requests.

Your ancestors are the number one spirits invested in your growth and wellbeing. They, more than anyone, want to help you, and you need them as well. Whenever you have a problem, who do you go to first? Your family! When you are happy, who do you call first? Your family! Just because they have died doesn't mean they no longer care. In fact, in death many of them are much more able to help you than when they were alive! So feel free to let your ancestors know about your life—what you are working on, what you are proud of. Let them know when you are scared and need their protection or when you need their guidance. Tell them when you are short on rent and ask if they can help. Burn candles to them when you ask, and say prayers for them.

Calling the Ancestors

Our ancestors are around us all the time, whether we've called them forth or not. However, the act of calling them forth really pulls them further into our world and helps them to interact with us. This process is simple. You light your ancestor candle and speak aloud something along the lines of "I call forth my ancestors, those who have found God on the other side and wish to guide and protect me in this lifetime. May they be here with me now, and all the days of my life." This does two things: First, it gives them permission to come forward and interact with us. Second, it specifies who exactly it is we are talking to. It can get dicey if we don't express exactly who we are speaking to on the other side. If we don't specify, just about anything can answer. So make sure to call forth the ancestors that are here for your "highest good." When you're done, thank them and extinguish the candle to close the session.

Praying for the Dead

One of the most important things that we can do for our ancestors is pray for them. We all have a good chunk of ances-tors who have made it to the Promised Land and are happily watching over us. However, there are also many ancestors that might not have gotten there for one reason or another. Sometimes spirits get lost or stuck on their way to the light. Sometimes they hold on to their anger, addictions, or fear, and it holds them back from joining God. Some are being pun-ished for their evil deeds. No matter the reason, our prayers can help them heal and find their way back to God.

The most common way to pray for the ancestors is to pray the rosary for all the souls trapped in purgatory. You may or may not believe in purgatory, but the metaphor remains relevant for attempting to help those who have been trapped on the other side. This includes but is not limited to our ancestors. You may also pray words from the heart, and I often go through a short list that isn't always the same but goes something like this, "I pray

Basically anyone who has died that has a connection to you in some way can be an ancestor, depending on how you approach it. I have also known people who create ancestor altars for their pets that have passed on.

There are many types of ancestors, including those in your bloodline going all the way back to the very first people.

for my ancestors who have not made it to God. If they are lost, let them be found. If they are scared, may they be brave. If they are damned, may they find deliverance. If they are stuck, may they be released. If they are wounded, may they be healed. If they are ready, may they find the light. If they are sorry, may they be forgiven." And so on and so forth.

Feeding the Ancestors

Feeding your ancestors is important! It's what sustains them, strengthens them, and helps anchor them in our world. I recommend feeding them at least once a week, if not more. This is done simply by calling them forth, placing a plate of food on their altar, and saying some prayers for them. You may also eat at the ancestor altar on special occasions—sharing a meal is a great way to connect with family! They also enjoy beverages such as coffee, liquor, and soda.

Elevating the Ancestors

Ancestor elevation works on a theory that the better standing our ancestors have in heaven, the better position they'll be in to watch over us, guide

us, and protect us. It is believed that through certain rituals we may be able to elevate the ancestors to new heights and therefore benefit ourselves here on earth.

You'll need:
9 thick books or bricks
1 white cloth
1 white novena candle
1 glass of water

Begin on the first day by placing the first book or brick on your ancestor altar and covering it with the white cloth. On top of the cloth place the lit white candle and the glass of water. Say prayers for the elevation of your ancestors. Pray that anything holding them back—regret, fear, their sins, etc.—be removed so that they may ascend higher. As you do this, imagine your prayers lifting them up higher and higher. Do this every day for nine days, adding a book or a brick each day. Eventually you'll have a small tower! At the end of the nine days, remove the bricks or books and store them away. You can repeat this as many times or as often as you would like.

Common Questions

Who counts as an ancestor?
There are many types of ancestors, including those in your bloodline going all the way back to the very first people. There are also our loved ones and friends who have passed on that we are not related to—these still count. Also there are ancestors of our trade. For instance, if you are a writer, the writers who came before are your ancestors as well. Basically anyone who has died that has a connection to you in some way can be an ancestor, depending on how you approach it. I have also known people who create ancestor altars for their pets that have passed on.

What if I don't know who my ancestors are?
This is fine too! You just pray to them as a unit, and they will hear you. I also highly recommend getting acquainted with online resources for genealogy research. It's fascinating, and with modern technology it's easier now than it ever has been to find out where we came from. Also if you have any living relatives, ask them for stories about your family, their parents and grandparents, etc. It's a great place to start.

What about my ancestors that were problematic? (Abusers, addicts, racists, etc.)
We all have jerks in our family tree. You can choose not to work with these ancestors; it's largely up to you. I do find sometimes, though, that some of these problematic ancestors have found healing on the other side and wish to make up for their misdeeds in life by acting as guides and helpers for us now. It's up to you whether or not you accept that help, but you should say prayers for them either way as it will contribute to their healing and yours as well. If they are acting up or becoming a menace, ask that your good ancestors deal with them on your behalf. They're usually more than happy to.

I'm adopted. Who do I pray to? My birth family? Or my adopted family?
Both! They might each wish to help guide and protect you in this life, or you may find that one line wants to work with you more or less than the other. Take some time to feel it out, and go with what is most comfortable for you.

—J. ALLEN CROSS

American Brujeria is available at redwheelweiser.com

J. Allen Cross is a practicing Witch of Mexican, Native American, and European descent whose craft was shaped by his Catholic upbringing and mixed family culture. Living in his home state of Oregon, he works as a psychic medium and occult specialist for a well-known paranormal investigation team out of the Portland metro area. When he's not investigating, he enjoys providing spells and potions to his local community, exploring haunted and abandoned places, working as a consultant for other workers and investigators, and of course writing about Witchcraft. Follow him on Instagram at @oregon_wood_witch.

MOON GARDENING

BY PHASE

Sow, transplant, bud and graft   *Plow, cultivate, weed and reap*

NEW	First Quarter	FULL	Last Quarter	NEW
Plant above-ground crops with outside seeds, flowering annuals.	Plant above-ground crops with inside seeds.	Plant root crops, bulbs, biennials, perennials.		Do not plant.

BY PLACE IN THE ZODIAC

In general—plant and transplant crops that bear above ground when the Moon is in a watery sign: Cancer, Scorpio or Pisces. Plant and transplant root crops when the Moon is in Taurus or Capricorn; the other earthy sign, Virgo, encourages rot. The airy signs, Gemini, Libra and Aquarius, are good for some crops and not for others. The fiery signs, Aries, Leo and Sagittarius, are barren signs for most crops and best used for weeding, pest control and cultivating the soil.

♈

Aries—*barren, hot and dry.* Favorable for planting and transplanting beets, onions and garlic, but unfavorable for all other crops. Good for weeding and pest control, for canning and preserving, and for all activities involving fire.

♉

Taurus—*fruitful, cold and dry.* Fertile, best for planting root crops and also very favorable for all transplanting as it encourages root growth. Good for planting crops that bear above ground and for canning and preserving. Prune in this sign to encourage root growth.

♊

Gemini—*barren, hot and moist.* The best sign for planting beans, which will bear more heavily. Unfavorable for other crops. Good for harvesting and for gathering herbs.

♋

Cancer—*fruitful, cold and moist.* Best for planting crops that bear above ground and very favorable for root crops. Dig garden beds when the Moon is in this sign, and everything planted in them will flourish. Prune in this sign to encourage growth.

♌

Leo—*barren, hot and dry.* Nothing should be planted or transplanted while the Moon is in the Lion. Favorable for weeding and pest control, for tilling and cultivating the soil, and for canning and preserving.

♍

Virgo—*barren, cold and dry.* Good for planting grasses and grains, but unfavorable for other crops. Unfavorable for canning and preserving, but favorable for weeding, pest control, tilling and cultivating. Make compost when the Moon is in the Virgin and it will ripen faster.

♎

Libra—*fruitful, hot and moist.* The best sign to plant flowers and vines and somewhat favorable for crops that bear above the ground. Prune in this sign to encourage flowering.

♏

Scorpio—*fruitful, cold and moist.* Very favorable to plant and transplant crops that bear above ground, and favorable for planting and transplanting root crops. Set out fruit trees when the Moon is in this sign and prune to encourage growth.

♐

Sagittarius—*barren, hot and dry.* Favorable for planting onions, garlic and cucumbers, but unfavorable for all other crops, and especially unfavorable for transplanting. Favorable for canning and preserving, for tilling and cultivating the soil, and for pruning to discourage growth.

♑

Capricorn—*fruitful, cold and dry.* Very favorable for planting and transplanting root crops, favorable for flowers, vines, and all crops that bear above ground. Plant trees, bushes and vines in this sign. Prune trees and vines to strengthen the branches.

♒

Aquarius—*barren, hot and moist.* Favorable for weeding and pest control, tilling and cultivating the soil, harvesting crops, and gathering herbs. Somewhat favorable for planting crops that bear above ground, but only in dry weather or the seeds will tend to rot.

♓

Pisces—*fruitful, cold and moist.* Very favorable for planting and transplanting crops that bear above ground and favorable for flowers and all root crops except potatoes. Prune when the Moon is in the Fishes to encourage growth. Plant trees, bushes and vines in this sign.

Consult our Moon Calendar pages for phase and place in the zodiac circle. The Moon remains in a sign for about two and a half days. Match your gardening activity to the day that follows the Moon's entry into that zodiacal sign. For best results, choose days when the phase and sign are both favorable. For example, plant seeds when the Moon is waxing in a suitable fruitful sign, and uproot stubborn weeds when the Moon is in the fourth quarter in a barren sign.

The MOON *Calendar*

is divided into zodiac signs rather than the more familiar Gregorian calendar.

2023   **2024**

 Bear in mind that new projects should be initiated when the Moon is waxing (from dark to full). When the Moon is on the wane (from full to dark), it is a time for storing energy and the wise person waits.

Please note that Moons are listed by day of entry into each sign. Quarters are marked, but as rising and setting times vary from one region to another, it is advisable to check your local newspaper, library or planetarium.
The Moon's Place is computed for Eastern Time.

aries

March 20 – April 19, 2023
Cardinal Sign of Fire ♈ Ruled by Mars ♂

ARIES

S	M	T	W	T	F	S
	Mar **20** Vernal Equinox Pisces	**21** Aries	**22** WAXING	**23**	**24** Taurus	**25** Make a plan
26 Pace yourself Gemini	**27**	**28** Cancer	**29**	**30**	**31** Light a flame Leo	April **1** All Fools' Day
2 Virgo	**3** Gather seeds in preparation	**4**	**5** Music brings joy Libra	**6** Seed Moon	**7** WANING Scorpio	**8** Vesak Day First planting
9 Begin a candle vigil Sagittarius	**10**	**11**	**12** Capricorn	**13**	**14** Ask the stars Aquarius	**15**
16 Beware of hungry ghosts Pisces	**17**	**18** Tame a fever Aries	**19**	**Basil,** *Ocimum basilicum*—**Scorpio/Mars** An herb in the mint family. Basil is an aromatic herb widely used in cooking, magic and healing. It is said that basil can be used in magic that involves luck,		

prosperity, protection and harmony. The Hindu Goddess Lakshmi has a strong affinity with basil. In one of her myths an enemy turned her into a basil plant! While she easily reverted to her original form, the basil plant retained some of her virtues such as abundance and good fortune. In the West basil is associated with prosperity. Sprinkling basil at the front door of a business will bring luck. Basil is said to help in death. Many European groups placed a sprig of basil in the hand of dead, so that they would have easy passage into the next world.

The Geomantic Figures: Fortuna Major

GEOMANCY IS AN ANCIENT SYSTEM of divination that uses sixteen symbols, the geomantic figures. Easy to learn and use, it was one of the most popular divination methods in the Middle Ages and Renaissance. It remained in use among rural cunning folk for many centuries thereafter, and is now undergoing a renaissance of its own as diviners discover its possibilities.

The geomantic figures are made up of single and double dots. Each figure has a name and a divinatory meaning, and the figures are also assigned to the four elements, the twelve signs of the Zodiac, the seven planets and the nodes of the Moon. The dots that make up the figures signify their inner meanings: the four lines of dots represent Fire, Air, Water and Earth, and show that the elements are present in either active (one dot) or latent (two dots) form.

The fifth of the geomantic figures is Fortuna Major, which means Greater Fortune. Fortuna Major belongs to the element of Fire, the Zodiacal sign Leo, and the Sun among the planets. Despite the fiery and solar symbolism of the figure, its pattern of dots resembles nothing so much as a valley through which a river flows—and this is a key to its meaning.

Read as symbols of the Elements, the dots that form Fortuna Major reveal much about the nature of this figure. In this figure the elements reverse their usual qualities: the active elements of Fire and Air are latent while the passive elements of Water and Earth are active.

In divination Fortuna Major stands for great good fortune. It can sometimes indicate difficulties at the beginning but triumph later on. In any reading having to do with a conflict or contest, it indicates victory. It represents success without struggle, that is the the success that comes from moving with the natural flow of events.

—JOHN MICHAEL GREER

taurus

April 20 – May 20, 2023

Fixed Sign of Earth ♉ Ruled by Venus ♀

S	M	T	W	T	F	S
Chamomile, *Matricaria recutita*—Leo/Sun Known for its purificatory and protective qualities, chamomile has been used magically since the time of ancient Egypt. Because of its bright yellow flower, it has been long associated with the Sun, prosperity and good luck. In fact, many a ⬇				April **20** ● Taurus	**21** Partial Solar Eclipse ⇦	**22** WAXING Gemini
23	**24**	**25** *Second planting* Cancer	**26**	**27** ◑ Leo	**28**	**29** *Light the fires*
30 Walpurgis Night Virgo	May **1** Beltane	**2** *Ride high* Libra	**3**	**4** *Visit the night sea* Scorpio	**5** ◯ Hare Moon	**6** Partial Lunar Eclipse ⇦
7 WANING Sagittarius	**8** White Lotus Day	**9** *Start fresh* Capricorn	**10**	**11** Aquarius	**12** ◐	**13** *Brew tea* Pisces
14 *Third planting*	**15** Aries	**16**	**17** Taurus	**18** *Scry into black earth*	**19** ●	**20** WAXING Gemini

gambler have washed their hands with chamomile infusions before playing at the table. Tapping its ability to purify and fortify, a chamomile rinse can be used to wash doors and windows thus guarding against unwelcome energies and keeping spirits from entering. Long called the Universal Condenser, an infusion of chamomile has been used to wash crystal balls and black mirrors before being used by the diviner.

SLOW GREEN LIGHTNING

EVERYONE appreciates a good sunset. Given the opportunity, many people will suspend mundane activities to witness this magical transformation from bright white to dim red to disappearance. If you're a Witch lucky enough to live where there's an unobstructed view of the western horizon, you may witness a rare and beautiful moment along with sunset if you know where to look. If the afternoon sky has been calm and cloudless, watch the sunset when it's time. You can usually glance at the area around the Sun without discomfort when the bottom of the Sun's disk touches the horizon. If conditions are right, just when the top of the disk descends below the horizon, a burst of green light will fill the space above the setting Sun.

That green light always exists in sunlight, but you can't see it because it's mixed in with all the other colors to make the intense white light you see during the day. You may remember the name "Roy G. Biv" as an acronym to list the wavelengths as colors of visible light in descending order of red, orange, yellow, green, blue, indigo and violet. For most of the day the shorter wavelengths of light—blue, indigo and violet—are scattered by the atmosphere, causing it to appear blue to us. As the Sun approaches the horizon, those colors start to be absorbed by the thickening atmosphere and the longer wavelengths—red, orange and yellow—start to show their characteristic sunset colors. Near the moment of sunset, the longer wavelengths also begin to be absorbed and green is left by itself for a moment. Scientists call this phenomenon the "green flash," but unlike a flash of lightning, it's slow enough that it could last a few seconds. Even so, don't blink or you really will miss it.

STELLUX

gemini

May 21 – June 20, 2023

Mutable Sign of Air ♎ Ruled by Mercury ☿

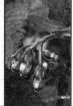

S	M	T	W	T	F	S
May **21**	**22** Love from within Cancer	**23**	**24** Leo	**25** Tigers know	**26**	**27** ◑ Virgo
28	**29** Oak Apple Day Libra	**30**	**31**	June **1** Scorpio	**2** Leave stress behind	**3** Dyad Moon Sagittarius
4 WANING	**5** Night of the Watchers Capricorn	**6**	**7** Read the cards Aquarius	**8**	**9** Pisces ◐	**10**
11 Aries	**12** Be proud of triumphs	**13**	**14** Taurus	**15**	**16** Encourage a friend Gemini	**17**
18 ● Cancer	**19** WAXING	**20** See the future				

Comfrey *Symphytum officinale*—Capricorn/ Saturn & Moon A true friend of the traveler and foe to the thief, sachets of comfrey leaves have been used as protective charms by many a traveler, as well as the well–placed sachet protecting luggage from loss and theft. Comfrey has long been associated with the Moon and the art of divination. In many recipes for Moon incense comfrey is a common herb, adding its distinctive scent. When scrying, Moon incense is an excellent mood setter. Comfrey can also be combined with mugwort to make a simple incense. To enhance dreams and promote relaxed sleep, many have used comfrey placed in the pillowcase. Comfrey also has been used as an herb of purification, used in baths and in potpourri to cleanse a room.

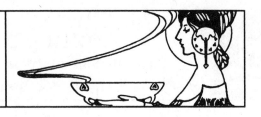

Mujadara

CERTAIN CROPS are tied to the prehistoric transformation of society from nomadic bands to settled farmers. Lentils are one of the eight founder crops around which settled civilization developed in the Near East (others include wheat, barley, vetches, peas and flax.) Cities arose almost immediately and within them unfolded all the *me*—the technologies of civilization ruled over by Inanna. In a touch of fascinating mystery, agriculture developed independently at roughly the same period in multiple places across the globe, within a few thousand years of one another—rice in East Asia, emmer and einkorn wheat in the Near East, potatoes and beans in South America, sugarcane in New Guinea, sorghum in Africa.

Millions of people living in the world now are directly descended from the very people who first learned the culinary magics, who first quickened seeds into crops, honey into mead, a campground into a city still inhabited thousands of years later. The next time you find yourself in the kitchen, honor the ancient mother who whispers in your ear.

Mujadara

This very old dish of onions, lentils and rice is found across the Middle East.

The cumin, lentils and onions are all foodstuffs eaten by the inhabitants of the Neolithic city Çatalhöyük, and of course rice is one of the ancient crops from other regions which has been adopted worldwide.

2-4 onions, thinly sliced
½ cup brown lentils
1 cup long grain rice, rinsed thoroughly
¼ cup olive oil
½ teaspoon salt
1 to 2 teaspoons black pepper
2 teaspoons cumin seeds (or 3/4 tsp ground)
1-2 cinnamon sticks (or a pinch ground)

Boil the lentils until soft but not mushy, then drain. Add onions to a pan on medium heat. When they just start to brown, add in the oil and spices, reduce heat and continue stirring until caramelized. Add rice and lentils to the pan with the caramelized onions, stirring gently to avoid breaking the grains. Add 1½ cups boiling water, turn the heat to medium high and cover. Bring to a boil, stir, cover and drop the heat to low. Simmer 17 minutes or until all water is absorbed. Remove from the heat and rest 5 minutes before uncovering. Fluff with a fork and serve.

—TONI FAIRCHILD

cancer

June 21 – July 22, 2023

Cardinal Sign of Water ▽ Ruled by Moon ☽

CANCER

S	M	T	W	T	F	S
Ginger, *Zingiber officinale—* **Scorpio/Mars** Being one of the first herbs imported to Europe from the Far East, the word spice was synonymous with ginger. Originating in the islands of the Pacific, it has been ↓			June **21** Summer Solstice Leo	**22** *Pick St. John's Wort*	**23** Virgo	**24** Midsummer
25 *Greet the Sun*	**26** Libra	**27**	**28** Scorpio	**29** *Fly by night*	**30** Sagittarius	July **1**
2 *Bond with your familiar*	**3** Mead Moon Capricorn	**4** WANING	**5** *Play a Witches' tune* Aquarius	**6**	**7** *Make a wish* Pisces	**8**
9 Aries	**10**	**11** *Offer a gift* Taurus	**12**	**13** *Use the sight* Gemini	**14**	**15**
16 *Reflect on a past life* Cancer	**17**	**18** WAXING Leo	**19**	**20** *Gaze into a purple candle's flame*	**21** Virgo	**22**

cultivated for more than 5000 years. To the practitioners of traditional medicine in Asia, ginger is considered a spice for the whole body. The ancient Romans held ginger to be the most efficacious of medicines it was used frequently to bestow fertility on couples. Used magically, ginger has varied uses such as a purifying agent, a strengthening additive and a cure for bad dreams. A pinch of ginger can be added to any herbal magic to add strength to the overall working.

TAROT'S THE WORLD

IN THE GAME OF TAROT the World trump is usually considered the mightiest trump of all and indeed the most powerful card in the entire Tarot deck. The World in this trump card is represented as a landscape with buildings—the material world in fact, which explains its title. This trump also includes a figure whose polygonal halo identifies her as a Virtue, standing on a wreath that surrounds the World's globe. She may well be Prudence, the fourth and last Cardinal Virtue, usually omitted from Tarot packs. In medieval symbolism Prudence was frequently portrayed holding a circular mirror in one hand in which she could view past, present and future, while in the other she grasps a serpent. To the moralizing theologian, Prudence was defined as knowledge of what was good, what was bad, and what was neither, deriving from memory of the past, intelligence about the present, and foresight into the future; in other words transcendent wisdom, something that would resonate well with the card's intimations of immortality. As to the trump's general interpretation in divination, it augurs the happiest of all happy endings and not surprisingly Tarot readers frequently consider it the best card in the deck.

Excerpted from Dame Fortune's Wheel Tarot—A Pictorial Key *by Paul Huson, published by The Witches' Almanac.*

leo

July 23 – August 22, 2023

Fixed Sign of Fire △ Ruled by Sun ☉

LEO

S	M	T	W	T	F	S
July 23 Ancient Egyptian New Year Libra	**24** *Count your blessings*	**25** ◑ Scorpio	**26**	**27** *Bless an object*	**28** Sagittarius	**29** *Harvest corn*
30 *Bake bread* Capricorn	**31** Lughnassad Eve	**Aug 1** ○ Wort Moon Aquarius	**2** WANING Lammas ⇦	**3** Pisces	**4** *Protect yourself*	**5** Aries
6	**7** Taurus	**8** ◐	**9** *Cast a spell* Gemini	**10**	**11** *Embrace twilight*	**12** Cancer
13 Diana's Day	**14** *Celebrate the Moon* Leo	**15** *Watch sunrise*	**16** ●	**17** WAXING Virgo	**18** Black Cat Appreciation Day ⇦	**19** Libra
20	**21** *Take your time*	**22** Scorpio				

Hyssop, *Hyssopus officinalis*—**Cancer/Jupiter** A member of the mint family, hyssop has been used in purification rites throughout the Mediterranean basin from time immemorial. Its purificatory properties have been extolled in mythology of the Levant as well as the scriptures of the Old Testament of the Bible. A bath with hyssop as the main ingredient is used to this very day by many magicians and Witches prior to ritual. Hyssop infused water for a floor wash is a great way of clearing a home of any negative influences. Carrying a satchel filled with hyssop and rue is great for protecting against jealousy and other negative energies. Amongst the magic workers of Sicily, hyssop is considered to be especially strong at repelling the evil eye.

Year of the Yin/Female Black Water Rabbit
January 22, 2023 – February 9, 2024

THROUGHOUT ASIA the Years of the Rabbit or Cat are much anticipated. The Rabbit evokes a comparatively peaceful cycle following the time of the troublesome Tiger. In some countries, including Japan, this year is attributed to the gentle house Cat. Creative urges, logical problem-solving, a kindly demeanor and clear-cut goals tend to make life more mild, orderly and comfortable. Sensible and suave, the congenial Rabbit (or Cat) wants comfort, quality and appreciation. Expectations to acquire the best of everything are often granted. One traditional tale about Rabbit's year belies this though. The Yin Black Water Rabbit year can mark a struggle for survival. There is a parable which focuses on a leaf caught in the current of a stream. The leaf is swept along, bumping into rocks and other obstacles as it continues its journey.

Genteel, reserved and scholarly, the Rabbit is considered a desirable birth sign. The Yin Water Rabbit is especially passive, idealistic and romantic. Rabbits are welcomed as wonderful choices as partners in marriage as well as in business relationships. Respected for artistic ability and sensitivity, Rabbit practices discretion in all things and seeks security. Those born in a Rabbit year are often gifted with exceptional longevity and a good share of wealth.

The Chinese astrology cycle follows a pattern of twelve years and five elements (Fire, Water, Wood, Metal and Earth). Every 60 years the element and animal pairs repeat. A counting system of 12 branches and 10 stems keeps track of whether the animal sign of the year is yin (female) or yang (male). Chinese New Year begins at the second New Moon following the Winter Solstice.

More information on the Water Rabbit can be found on our website at
http://TheWitchesAlmanac.com/pages/almanac-extras

Years of the Dog
1951, 1963, 1975, 1987, 1999, 2011, 2023

Illustration by Ogmios MacMerlin

virgo

August 23 – September 22, 2023
Mutable Sign of Earth ♍ Ruled by Mercury ☿

S	M	T	W	T	F	S
Lavender, *Lavandula angustifolia*—**Gemini/Mercury** At birth as well as at death lavender's many uses have been known since the time of the ancients. Preparing the dead for the afterlife, the priests of ancient ↓			Aug **23**	**24** Sagittarius	**25**	**26** *Fashion an incense* Capricorn
27 *Open your eyes*	**28** Aquarius	**29** *Howl at the Moon*	**30** Barley Moon Pisces	**31** WANING	Sept **1** *Give and take* Aries	**2**
3 Taurus	**4**	**5** *Support an endeavor*	**6** Gemini	**7**	**8** *Cast the runes* Cancer	**9**
10 *Face a fear* Leo	**11**	**12**	**13** *Do not fear* Virgo	**14**	**15** WAXING	**16** *Sing to the birds* Libra
17 Ganesh Chaturthi ⇨	**18** *Ask for guidance* Scorpio	**19**	**20** Sagittarius	**21** *Gaze at the stars*	**22**	

Egypt used lavender as an ingredient during mummification. Lavender was given to women in labor. Squeezing the bundle during contractions would release the scent, known to calm the mind and ease pain. The name lavender comes form the Latin verb *lavare*, which means "to wash." Quite appropriate as lavender oil is often added to baths to cleanse and sanctify the body and the soul! Known as spikenard in the Levant, it was one of eleven sacred herbs used in making the incense used in the Temple of Jerusalem.

The Bundle of Sticks

A CERTAIN FATHER had a family of sons, who were forever quarreling among themselves. No words he could say did the least good, so he cast about in his mind for some very striking example that should make them see that discord would lead them to misfortune.

One day when the quarreling had been much more violent than usual and each of the sons was moping in a surly manner, he asked one of them to bring him a bundle of sticks. Then handing the bundle to each of his Sons in turn he told them to try to break it. Although each one tried his best, none was able to do so.

The father then untied the bundle and gave the sticks to his Sons to break one by one. This they did very easily.

"My sons," said the father, "do you not see how certain it is that if you agree with each other and help each other, it will be impossible for your enemies to injure you? But if you are divided among yourselves, you will be no stronger than a single stick in that bundle."

Moral: In unity is strength.

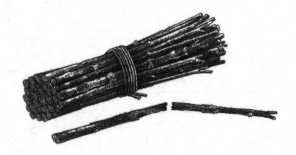

libra

September 23 – October 22, 2023
Cardinal Sign of Air ♎ Ruled by Venus ♀

LIBRA

S	M	T	W	T	F	S
Mugwort, *Artemisia vulgaris*—**Libra/Moon** Psychic visions have long been associated with the Moon and her Goddesses. Artemisia vulgaris was named in honor of the Goddess Artemis. As well as wormwood, it is well known to induce psychic states. Mugwort can be found the world over. In folk customs of Europe it was said to be used by Witches so that they might travel ↓						Sept **23** Autumnal Equinox Capricorn
24	**25** Aquarius	**26**	**27** *Visit the past* Pisces	**28**	**29** (Blood Moon) Aries	**30** WANING
Oct **1** Taurus	**2**	**3** *Notice others* Gemini	**4**	**5** Cancer	**6**	**7**
8 Leo	**9**	**10** Virgo	**11** *Spin the wheel*	**12**	**13** Partial Solar Eclipse ⇨ Libra	**14**
15 WAXING Scorpio	**16**	**17**	**18** Sagittarius	**19** *Enjoy fine wine*	**20** Capricorn	**21**
22 Aquarius	in the spirit world. In the Americas some indigenous peoples burn mugwort to purify their sacred precincts. In Asia it was used to ward off evil spirits. Mugwort has also been widely used in conjunction with divination and lucid dreaming. To reap the benefit of mugwort it can be burned, put into satchels, infused in a tea or steeped in oil and used for anointing the third eye.					

⋛ Ash ⋚

Nion

LIKE THE birch and the rowan, the ash tree thrives high up on exposed hills. The tree is easily recognized by its pure gray bark and large spreading crown especially after its leaves have fallen. The ash comes to leaf as late as May and loses its leaves by early October.

The Greeks dedicated the ash tree to Poseidon, God of the sea, and sailors carried its wood as protection against the threat of drowning. The major spiritual significance of the ash tree comes from Northern Europe, where as *Yggdrasil*, the World Tree, it connects the Underworld, Earth and Heaven. The ash is associated in Norse myths with Odin (Woden,) supreme among gods, who sought to increase his wisdom with extreme suffering. It was on an ash tree that he hanged himself:

Nine whole nights on a
wind-rocked tree,
Wounded with a spear,
I was offered to Odin,
myself to myself,
On that tree that none
may ever know
What root beneath it runs.

This account is recorded in the *Elder Edda*, Icelandic poems dating from about the tenth century.

Ash keys, so-called because they resemble keys used in medieval locks, are the winged seed pods dispersed by winter winds to form new trees. They are of value as fertility charms. Ash is one of the few woods that will burn easily and steadily when still green. Divination fires are often of green ash.

scorpio

October 23 – November 21, 2023

Fixed Sign of Water ▽ Ruled by Pluto ♀

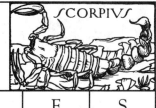

SCORPIUS

S	M	T	W	T	F	S
	Oct 23	24	25	26	27 Partial Lunar Eclipse ⇨	28 Snow Moon
		Pisces	*Buy a pumpkin*	Aries		Taurus
29 WANING	30 *Invite the ghosts* Gemini	31 Samhain Eve	Nov 1 Hallowmas	2 *Honor the dead* Cancer	3	4 Leo
5 ◐	6	7 *Stock your herbal pantry* Virgo	8 *Light a candle*	9 Libra	10 *Ask the spirit board*	11
12 *Let go of fears* Scorpio	13 ●	14 WAXING Sagittarius	15 *Make a deep wish*	16 Hecate Night Capricorn	17	18 *Gather colorful leaves* Aquarius
19	20 ◑ Pisces	21				

Primrose, *Primula vulgaris***—Libra/Moon** A favored shelter of Fairies, Primrose has been traditionally employed for courting the favor, blessing and presence of the Fey Folk. In fact, it has been said that if you wish to see Fairies, you should eat primrose flowers. Hanging a sprig of primrose at the door is an invitation for them to enter your home. Primrose is associated with love as well as with those who do not know love. In times past, if a young woman died before she married, a garland of primrose was put at the door, the flowers were allowed to fall off and then it was buried in the graveyard. It was also customary to cover the bed of newly-wedded couples with primrose flowers. Primrose has long been a symbol of love and youth. Unsurprisingly it has a history of use during Beltane for garlands. It is said that the Norse Goddess Freya had a special liking of primrose.

 # TALISMAN

THE HORSESHOE

THE ORIGINS of using horseshoes as talismans has been lost in the mists of time. Shoeing horses has been employed for almost as long as mankind has ridden this very noble beast. The earliest archeological records of shoeing horses were found in the Eurasian steppe where woven plants were used to protect their hooves. It was perhaps the advent of the paved road that saw the use of metals for horseshoes. Some historians have implied that it was the Chaldeans who first used metals, other have asserted that it was the Romans. The use of iron for horseshoes may have been commonplace by sometime after 100 BCE.

The good luck and protective properties associated with horseshoes is very much interlaced with the iron from which the shoe is fashioned and the craftsman magician—the blacksmith—who commits this magical act. The very act of forging by fire is believed to purify and strengthen iron.

The horseshoe has very much been associated with warding the home from attack by goblins and fairies due of their inability to deal with the presence of iron. Hung above the doorways leading into a home, the peskiest of goblin and sprite will be prohibited from entering. The upright hung horseshoe is also said to bring luck to the householders and their guests. There are many who believe that to retain the good luck bestowed by the horseshoe, you must exit by the same door by which you entered.

It is also said that carrying a horseshoe on your person is an excellent way to protect yourself while traveling through your day. In times past, the fashioning of small iron horseshoes to carry in a pocket or a purse was not uncommon. In fact, many a bride has a small horseshoe sewn into the hem of her wedding dress to impart good luck to the union. Finally, sleeping with a horseshoe under the pillow on New Year's Eve is believed to impart luck on the individual for the coming year.

—DEVON STRONG

sagittarius
November 22 – December 21, 2023
Mutable Sign of Fire △ Ruled by Jupiter ♃

S	M	T	W	T	F	S
Rue, *Ruta graveolens*—Libra/ **Moon** A common ingredient in magic and spell-making during the Middle Ages, rue was traditionally hung in doorways and windows to keep the home safe from evil that might ↓			Nov **22**	**23** *Begin a new project* Aries	**24**	**25** Taurus
26	**27** Oak Moon Gemini	**28** WANING	**29** *Be kind* Cancer	**30**	Dec **1** *Eat an apple* Leo	**2**
3 *Support a friend*	**4** Virgo	**5** 🌓	**6** Libra	**7** *Listen to the wind*	**8**	**9** *Cast a spell* Scorpio
10	**11** *Write a story* Sagittarius	**12** ⚫	**13** WAXING Capricorn	**14** *Offer compliments*	**15**	**16** Fairy Queen Eve Aquarius
17 Saturnalia	**18** *Blow a kiss* Pisces	**19** 🌗	**20** *Take cover!* Aries	**21** *Light the Yule log*		

enter. It is an herb that has strong connections with both Diana and Aradia, being sacred to both. Rue can be used to protect any home by using the plant as an aspergillum to scatter water in each room. The Romans valued the powerful protective qualities of rue. The modern-day inheritors of Rome, Italians have long had the cimaruta, a folk talisman to ward off evil eye and a protection for babies. The silver pendant is a silver sprig of rue with various charms—Sun, Moon, key, etc.—at the end of each branch.

Came the voice of Destiny,
calling o'er the Ionian Sea,
"The Great God Pan is dead, is dead
Humbled is the horned head;
shut the door that hath no key—
waste the vales of Arcady."

Shackled by the Iron Age,
lost the woodland heritage,
heavy goes the heart of man,
parted from the light-foot Pan;
wearily he wears the chain
till the Goat-god comes again.

Half a man and half a beast,
Pan is greatest, Pan is least.

Pan is all, and all is Pan;
Look for him in every-man;
goat-hoof swift and shaggy thigh—
follow him to Arcady.

He shall wake the living dead—
cloven hoof and horned head,
human heart and human brain,
Pan the goat-god comes again!
Half a beast and half a man-
Pan is all, and all is Pan.

Come, O Goat-god, come again!

From The Rite of Pan as found in
The Goat-Foot God,
DION FORTUNE

capricorn

December 21 2023 – January 19, 2024
Cardinal Sign of Earth ▽ Ruled by Saturn ♄

S	M	T	W	T	F	S
Sage, *Salvia officinalis*—**Sagittarius/Jupiter** Common in the kitchen, apothecary and Witches' cabinet, sage is one of the most known and used herbs—in ancient times and modern. A true plant of Jupiter, sage is associated with wisdom, protection and good luck. In Roman times the gathering ↓				Dec **21** Winter Solstice	**22** *Count snowflakes* Taurus	**23**
24 *Light a yellow candle* Gemini	**25**	**26** Wolf Moon Cancer	**27** WANING	**28** *Cheer up!*	**29** Leo	**30** *Release*
31 Virgo	Jan **1** *Pray to your Gods*	**2**	**3** Libra	**4** *Count your successes*	**5** Scorpio	**6**
7 *Enjoy a winter fire*	**8** Sagittarius	**9** Feast of Janus	**10** *Work Earth magic* Capricorn	**11**	**12** WAXING Aquarius	**13**
14 *See natural beauty* Pisces	**15**	**16** *Avoid greed* Aries	**17**	**18** *Accept hard times* Taurus	**19**	

of sage was a sacred event in honor of Jove. In Rome as well as the rest of Europe, sage was said to impart long life. There is an Italian proverb extolling sage: "Why should a man die whilst sage grows in his garden, if not because nothing can stand against death?" Both the Romans and the Greeks believed that eating sage would improve the mind, promote wisdom and aid in memory. Of course, the burning of sage has been used in many societies to create serenity and purity in any home or temple.

Notable Quotations

EARTH

The fairest thing in nature, a flower, still has its roots in earth and manure.

D. H. Lawrence

The whole earth is the tomb of heroic men and their story is not given only on stone over their clay but abides everywhere without visible symbol woven into the stuff of other mens lives.

Pericles

You carry Mother Earth within you. She is not outside of you. Mother Earth is not just your environment. In that insight of inter-being, it is possible to have real communication with the Earth, which is the highest form of prayer.

Thich Nhat Hanh

The earth is the mother of all people, and all people should have equal rights upon it.

Chief Joseph

It suddenly struck me that that tiny pea, pretty and blue, was the Earth. I put up my thumb and shut one eye, and my thumb blotted out the planet Earth. I didn't feel like a giant. I felt very, very small.

Neil Armstrong

We are going to inherit the earth; there is not the slightest doubt about that.

Buenaventura Durruti

The poetry of the earth is never dead.

John Keats

From the dust of the earth, from the common elementary fund, the Creator has made Homo sapiens. From the same material he has made every other creature, however noxious and insignificant to us. They are earth-born companions and our fellow mortals.

John Muir

Quotes compiled by Isabel Kunkle.

aquarius

January 20 – February 18, 2024

Fixed Sign of Air △ Ruled by Uranus ♅

S	M	T	W	T	F	S
Marjoram, *Origanum majorana*—**Aries/Mercury** Found in many savory recipes, Greek mythology tells us that marjoram was cultivated by Aphrodite. Many would say that it is for this very reason that a truly effective love potion could not be made without it. For those questing for matters of the heart, it was said that a pillow made with a stuffing of marjoram would reveal ↓					Jan **20** Gemini	
21 *Cloud gaze*	**22**	**23** Cancer	**24** *Turn the tide*	**25** Storm Moon Leo	**26** WANING	**27**
28 Virgo	**29** *Clouds gather*	**30** Libra	**31** *Use a pendulum to decide*	Feb **1** Oimelc Eve	**2** Scorpio	**3** Candlemas ⇦
4 Sagittarius	**5** *Break a rule*	**6** Capricorn	**7**	**8** *Try something new* Aquarius	**9**	**10** Chinese New Year WAXING Pisces
11	**12**	**13** *Climb higher* Aries	**14**	**15** Lupercalia Taurus	**16**	**17** *Strike a foe* Gemini
18	the true love of the dreamer. In ancient Greece young couples would wear wreaths of marjoram on their wedding night. Marjoram has also been used as a remedy to impart happiness and banish sadness. A pulverized bit of the herb can be placed in the four corners of each room of a house to affect the change. A bath for seven days in an infusion of marjoram has been used to bring happiness and blessings into the life of the afflicted.					

Of a Neophyte, and How the Black Art Was Revealed
unto Him By the Fiend Asomuel

Aubrey Beardsley

pisces

February 19 – March 20, 2024
Mutable Sign of Water ▽ Ruled by Neptune Ψ

S	M	T	W	T	F	S
	Feb 19 Meditate Cancer	20	21 Heal with your hands Leo	22	23 Concentrate	24 Chaste Moon Virgo
25 WANING	26 Paint with color Libra	27	28 Music heals	29 LEAP DAY Scorpio	Mar 1 Matronalia	2 Sagittarius
3	4	5 Capricorn	6 Contact an old friend	7 Aquarius	8	9 Measure karma Pisces
10	11 WAXING Aries	12	13 Plan your garden Taurus	14	15 Movement frees Gemini	16
17 Cancer	18 Calm before the storm	19 Minerva's Day	20 Leo			

Vervain, *Verbena officinalis*— **Gemini/Venus** Hippocrates tells us that vervain can alleviate sterility in women and Galen tells us that it will "strengthen the member." Vervain has been used magically by the ancients of Egypt, Rome, Greece and the Celtic lands. It was used by all these societies to ward against evil and negative energy, as well as being a purifying agent for ritual implements. Vervain was used in rituals of both Thor and Jupiter, using an infusion to sprinkle the altar of either. Long a charm against headaches and snakebites, a fresh sprig of vervain was carried to ensure protection. It is said that a drink made of vervain was used in the rituals of the Druids, allowing them to connect with the ancestors and the Underworld.

ÒGÚN

The Immortal Dressed in Palm Fronds

THE YORUBA of Southwestern Nigeria have long revered a complex of deities known as Orìṣá, that can embody the most primordial of forces and instincts while also expressing the highest of ideals. It is among the innumerable Irúnmolè or primary emanations of the high God Òlódùmaré that we encounter the forces that created and sustain this green planet while also acting to dispatch, replace or destroy anything that has succumbed to inertia. The pantheon of the Yoruba has long accommodated the sense of divinity of both creation and destruction.

It is in the Orìṣá ÒGÚN that we encounter a powerful hunter, warrior, blacksmith deity who truly exemplifies the extremes—creator of innovation and benefactor as well as fearsome, bloodthirsty avenger and keeper of oaths. These qualities are laid bare in the *Oríkì* (praise poetry) that is sung to ÒGÚN by his devotees. He is extolled as a chief among the deities, one who uses his machete to prepare the farm and to clear the roads. He is an honest deity, the owner of truth and witness to oaths. In the very same Oríkì he

is praised as the deity who bathes in blood rather than water, the fearsome Orìṣá who inhabits the battlefield and notably we are warned that any who make jest of warfare will suffer his wrath. All are vigorously warned that any Orìṣá or human who ill regards ÒGÚN will eat with their hands—suffer the loss of technology. And finally, in ÒGÚN's praise songs we are reminded that he is the epitome of the loner who will quit his solitude to heed the righteous call to arms leading both human and immortal alike.

Creator and destroyer

It is Òlódùmaré who created the cosmos and the Orìṣá, and it is Obàtálá who created the Earth and subsequently human beings. They both embody functional creativity in as much as theirs is the creation of segments of the physical plane. ÒGÚN, however, embodies the creativity that arises out of art—be it the crafting of objects or the creativity of fine song and poetry. As example, one of the finest poetic forms of the Yoruba is poetry attributed to ÒGÚN and his worshippers, *Ìjálá*. This lyrical poetic artform extolls the vir-

tues of the deities in addition to attesting to the wonders of the natural world. Ògún has also been the Orìṣá technological innovation such as the fashioning of tools that lead to the progress of mankind.

Without diminishing his continued creativity in the world, Ògún is also the divinity who has embodied destructive forces. He is seen as being one of the "hottest" of the Orìṣá—he is easily incited. While there are at times just ends in armed conflict, it is never without blood, death and destruction. As already stated, Ògún is said to bathe in blood—the implication is that he is the consummate warrior, unafraid and acting at all times with abandon. Ògún's red hot anger is not always seen as just or necessary when unleashed, though. In such cases when Ògún disengages from the state of agitation there is often recompense for his actions.

Ògún's anger is remembered in one such incident that resulted in the death of innocents. Ògún decided to return to the city of Iré, a city that he once ruled. In his place, his son had long ruled over the city in a time known for its peace. On his arrival in Iré he encountered the citizens celebrating a festival. He was hungry, thirsty and tired from his long journey.

Because he was dirty from his journey and because he had not been to Iré in such a long time, none recognized him nor offered him hospitality. In his long absence, he no longer knew the chiefs and his son was not to be found. Of course—as is usual for Ògún—his patience was short and his anger began to show. His anger soon became blind rage. He began to wreak havoc—he began decapitating any in his path. Hearing the red-hot shrieking, Ògún's son at a distance immediately recognized that it was his father and that he had been incited to the point of blind destruction. He immediately made his way to Ògún and offered him the foods he traditionally ate: he wet Ògún's tongue with palm oil and put a jar of palm wine to his mouth.

Being propitiated with the proper food and drink, Ògún immediately began to return to a calm state. He looked around, surveying the destruction that he had caused and at once was filled with sadness and remorse. In fact, so distraught was he that he lowered his arm and pointed his cutlass at the ground. Uttering an incantation, with a terrifying groan the ground opened. Before disappearing into the Earth, he instructed his son and the people of Iré that they could call on him

with certain words in their time of need. He warned them that they should not call on him unless there was indeed an enemy before them, lest he destroy them instead.

Clothed in palm fronds he hunts

Ògún's oldest profession is that of the hunter. So strong is his association with the hunt that his dominion extends to the forests and the mountains where hunting takes place. It in Ògún the hunter that we encounter the quality that is the quintessential loner. More often than not, hunting is a solitary profession, especially in a society that is both heavily agrarian while also being cosmopolitan. Hunters are walkers of liminal territories. Their interest is at once both mysterious and mundane. The hunter becomes one with their prey. They, like animals, must be able to stalk without being detected. It is from Ògún that hunters get their strong medicine for hunting.

There is not a hunter that would leave his home without some of the most sacred objects of Ògún—fresh palm kernels and palm fronds. Like many of the Orìṣà (especially Èṣù and Ifá), the palm tree has a special place in Ògún's lore. Equally it is important for the hunter, providing palm oil for cooking and palm wine for refreshing the throat. The palm kernels are fuel for fires and the fronds are his clothing while hunting. He would also carry little bits of metal in addition to his spear or arrow tips and these days shotgun or gun. With all these items, the hunters is assured success.

All of the above are objects that are considered essential to the worship of Ògún. It is by palm oil and palm wine that Ògún is cooled down. Palm kernels would be used in the smithy as fuel to fashion the iron implements that decorate a shrine to Ògún. Palm fronds decorate his shrines, and if encountered on a path will indicate that there is a shrine of a divinity ahead. In a true dichotomous fashion, when we consider his connection with iron and hunting, Ògún is a divinity of both wilderness and civilization.

Master of iron and the forge

It is in Ògún the Orìṣà of iron, metallurgy and the forge that we encounter a divinity of technology. So integrated is Ògún's association with iron that the spirit of iron is Ògún. He is more than a divinity that has rulership over iron. There is no distinction between iron and Ògún. To touch iron is to touch and be touched by Ògún.

Ògún is present in all the processes of iron, from its extraction from the ground to the fashioning of tools and finally to the use of the tools and how iron continues to drive innovation in human society at all levels.

While Ògún may not be the patron of various professions, he is present in many because of the tools used in each. Without iron the work of farmers, hunters, warriors, carpenters, surgeons etc., would be impossible. Ògún's influence is not limited to the tools that he provides for various professions. It is said that Ògún does not rest and it is often noted that he brings a high level of ethics to his tasks and expects that all should do the same.

The first mystery of iron is that of the mining of ore from the ground and the extraction of iron from the raw stone. The process was a closely guarded secret of the "children" of Ògún. The smelting process has quite obviously been associated with transformation not only of stone but also of man. The worker-priest who was able to instigate the purification process of ore could certainly do the same for the afflicted client. It is in this capacity that the priest of Ògún acts as the agent of purification of the soul.

As the divine blacksmith, Ògún truly becomes the conveyer of societal progress. As already stated, the work of the forge touches so many constituent professions within society. Blacksmiths are responsible for the creation of tools, agricultural implements, weapons and important regalia used by many priesthoods as well as their medicine which is employed in the creation of protective amulets for the general population as well as for hunters.

It is at the forge that we again encounter the dual nature of Ògún. Without the tools that he has provided for the nurturing of social progress—the various technologies whereby growth is facilitated—humanity would not have achieved such heights. Ògún's tools have allowed mankind to not only till the Earth but also remove the tumor. In the same breath, it is by the forge that weapons of war were created, allowing for society to show its ignoble proclivity towards subjugation. Equally, the blacksmith has been employed to create amulets that help to clear the path of difficulties before the client or allow for retribution on the undeserving enemy.

The cleansing waters

It is the magic of the forge that puts the blacksmiths, and by extension priests of Ògún, in a unique position as social purifiers. In addition to smithing, as already discussed hunting and war are both activities that are ruled by Ògún. He is seen to be the supreme hunter and the consummate warrior. Both of these activities require contact with death and blood—they are necessarily acts of aggression.

The men who live the life of a warrior or a hunter share in status as they are praised for their acts of bravery. They are in many ways the saviors of the communities that they live in. They provide for security (physical and food) of the larger population. Their valor puts them at risk not only for their own lives but also they incur blood debt by killing a fierce animal or enemy. Hunters and warriors run the risk that the heat and bloodshed of the battle or hunt will cause disorder, "cooking" his head. Hunting and killing require a cleansing before reintegration into society.

It is believed that only Ògún has the right to take life, be it human or animal. Those who take life by means of Ògún's tools must be cleansed of the blood and it is by the waters that the blacksmith uses to quench iron that man is cleansed. Cool water is said to cool iron and the head equally. The water from forges is used to cleanse the head of the warriors and hunters as well as their weapons. In fact, so strong is the medicine of water from the forge that is used to cleanse Ògún's objects in his shrines.

One final cleansing that is enacted by the waters of the forge is the cleaning of implements used to make sacrificial offerings to the Orìṣá. It is understood by all priesthoods that while the first Orìṣá to be sung to and propitiated is always Èṣú, it is actually Ògún whose thirst is quenched first by means of the sacrificial knife— all knives being an extension of him. Just as the warrior/hunter are purified, the hands, knife and the animal are relieved of their heat with cool water directly after sacrifice.

The iron cutlass clears all

Ògún is the Orìṣá who is said to clear all obstacles. His most treasured of tools, the cutlas, can be used for hunting as well as for tilling the field. It can also be used to cut through the most dense of forests or situations. Many a believer have come before a shrine to Ògún seeking relief from the many obstacles that life has put in their path. In the distant past, the Orìṣá also sought out Ògún to clear the path ahead of them. In one particular tale, the other divinities sought the help of Ògún.

We are told that in a time long ago the Orìṣá inhabited Ile Ife, the land first made by Obàtálá. They lived side by side with the humans that were also created by Obàtálá. They farmed and hunted— tending to both with implements made of wood, stone and soft metal. In time Ife was overwhelmed with the population of divinities, humans and animals. More land was needed.

Recognizing that something needed to be done, the divinities met to decide how to proceed. It was decided that they would first need to clear some of the land of forest that grew around them, knowing that they could then increase the land available for cultivation.

The first to venture out to clear the forest was Òsanyin, the divinity of herbs and healing. He went to the edge of the forest to begin his work. He was not long working on clearing the forest when his blade bent and was unusable. He returned to the town and told the others that he indeed began the job but could not finish as his blade was bent before too long.

The next volunteer to go out to clear the forests was Orìṣá Okó, the divinity of farming. He too went to the edge of the forest to begin his work and like Òsanyin he was not too long working as his blade was also bent and made unusable. He returned to town and told the others he could not finish the job as his blade was also bent before long.

Èṣú volunteered next, assuring all that he would certainly be able to clear the forest. He went to the edge of the forest and began his work in earnest. He indeed was able to make more headway than the two before him, however his blade also was bent before long. He returned to the town and told the others that he was indeed able to make more progress than those before him, but in the end his blade, too, bent.

One by one all the Orìṣá went to the forest, trying to clear it and one by one they were unsuccessful because their blades were not strong enough—until at last they asked Ògún for help. He ventured out the next day to the edge of the forest. He took out his iron cutlas and began to clear the forest, not stopping until the night.

He returned to the town with his straight, sharp blade glistening in the moonlight. The others were awed by the amount accomplished by Ògún and that his blade was so strong. Ògún shared with them the secret of iron that he had been gifted by Òlódùmaré. He set up a forge and gifted each with a new, sharp cutlass.

The shrine of Ògún

Because of his various associations, shrines to Ògún are varied from region to region and from house to house. In almost all instances—in keeping with his wild uncontainable energy—his shrines are kept at the very least outdoors. In some instances, his shrine is kept in a wooded or wild area of a family compound. It is very common to find miniature hunting implements in his shrine and palm fronds also play an important role. Some localities will have his shrine covered with dried frond skirts so that the contents of the shrine can only be seen when they are removed. In many areas of Yorubaland, the most important component of his shrines is iron in both its raw state and fashioned implements. The content of his shrines will be dictated by the region where they are found—among the Fon, Yoruba, Benin, etc. Ògún's cult, like a number of Orişá, has been spread across the Atlantic to Brazil, Haiti, Cuba, etc. In the Americas his shrine is often contained in a small cauldron. The chief implement is usually an anvil. In some

areas of Brazil, his shrine is simply a slab of iron.

The witness of oaths

Ògún is known to be the divinity of truthfulness and integrity. He is said to bring down his wrath of those who are liars or thieves or in some way have a lack of integrity. It is by Ògún that many an oath is sworn. It is not uncommon for a king to swear fealty to his people by placing his hand on a cutlas, a sword or a piece of iron. In fact, many old coronation rites in Yorubaland have this as an integral part of proceedings.

Swearing by Ògún is so embedded in the Yoruba psyche that the British, in their occupation of West African lands, began to accept testimony that was sworn before the court on a piece of iron. While it fell out of favor for a bit of time, this custom and other indigenous ethical practices are beginning to make their way back as cultural norms. In fact, a recent military governor of Ogun State, Nigeria insisted that his oath of office be taken on a cutlass symbolizing Ògún.

May Ògún accompany you on your path, be it sylvan or paved highway. May he provide you with protection and ability and courage.

—IFADOYIN SANGOMUYIWA

Ìjà tí n ó jà yí kími níyì síí.

Àjàgbuyì níti kìnìún.

Àjàgbuyì níti Ààrá.

Òisùndá. Ìwọ ló ńdá wọn ni'jàkádì

lójọ́ gbogbo nílẹ̀kílẹ̀

Ìjà tí n ó jà yí kími níyì síí.

Àjàgbuyì.

May the battle I fight always add to my honor.

The battle that brings honor belongs to the lion.

The battle that brings honor belongs to Ààrá.

Òisùndá. You defeated them in struggle everyday

and everywhere.

May the battle I fight always add to my honor,

the battle that brings honor.

Excerpt from Òisùndá Wọ́nrín Divination Poem

The Gifting Feather

GIFTING is an old custom. It is not like giving a birthday, holiday or wedding present. It can either be a planned event or a spontaneous gesture. Gifting expresses an intent to honor a person or situation with a unique token charged with the energy of Spirit. When the Great Spirit or the Old Gods whisper, then it is time to gift another. A beautiful feather is a desirable choice. All ages and all kinds of people can enjoy and appreciate this unique gift. The appearance of fallen feathers suggests associations with angel wings and messages or omens from the heavenly realms. The type of bird from which the feather fell or its color can hint at an omen or other messages. Wrapping the base or shaft of the feather with colorful fiber and then adding additional ribbons, beads or other tokens can embellish the gifting feather. Its message is a reminder to make wise choices. At the proper time the gifting feather can be thoughtfully passed along to another. The true value and power carried by the gifting feather is realized when it is regifted.

—DIKKI-JO MULLEN

2023 SUNRISE AND SUNSET TIMES
Providence—San Francisco—Sydney—London

	Sunrise				Sunset			
	Prov	SF	Syd	Lon	Prov	SF	Syd	Lon
Jan 5	7:14 AM	7:26 AM	5:51 AM	8:06 AM	4:28 PM	5:04 PM	8:08 PM	4:05 PM
15	7:11 AM	7:24 AM	6:00 AM	8:00 AM	4:38 PM	5:13 PM	8:07 PM	4:19 PM
25	7:05 AM	7:19 AM	6:10 AM	7:49 AM	4:50 PM	5:24 PM	8:04 PM	4:36 PM
Feb 5	6:54 AM	7:10 AM	6:21 AM	7:33 AM	5:04 PM	5:36 PM	7:56 PM	4:55 PM
15	6:42 AM	7:00 AM	6:30 AM	7:15 AM	5:17 PM	5:47 PM	7:47 PM	5:14 PM
25	6:27 AM	6:47 AM	6:39 AM	6:55 AM	5:30 PM	5:58 PM	7:36 PM	5:32 PM
Mar 5	6:15 AM	6:36 AM	6:46 AM	6:38 AM	5:39 PM	6:06 PM	7:26 PM	5:46 PM
15	6:58 AM	7:21 AM	6:54 AM	6:16 AM	6:51 PM	7:15 PM	7:13 PM	6:03 PM
25	6:41 AM	7:06 AM	7:02 AM	5:53 AM	7:02 PM	7:25 PM	6:59 PM	6:20 PM
Apr 5	6:23 AM	6:50 AM	6:10 AM	6:28 AM	7:14 PM	7:35 PM	5:44 PM	7:38 PM
15	6:06 AM	6:35 AM	6:18 AM	6:06 AM	7:25 PM	7:44 PM	5:32 PM	7:55 PM
25	5:51 AM	6:22 AM	6:25 AM	5:45 AM	7:36 PM	7:53 PM	5:20 PM	8:12 PM
May 5	5:38 AM	6:10 AM	6:33 AM	5:26 AM	7:47 PM	8:02 PM	5:10 PM	8:28 PM
15	5:27 AM	6:01 AM	6:40 AM	5:10 AM	7:57 PM	8:11 PM	5:02 PM	8:44 PM
25	5:18 AM	5:53 AM	6:47 AM	4:57 AM	8:07 PM	8:19 PM	4:56 PM	8:58 PM
June 5	5:12 AM	5:49 AM	6:54 AM	4:47 AM	8:15 PM	8:27 PM	4:52 PM	9:10 PM
15	5:11 AM	5:48 AM	6:58 AM	4:44 AM	8:21 PM	8:32 PM	4:52 PM	9:18 PM
25	5:13 AM	5:50 AM	7:01 AM	4:45 AM	8:23 PM	8:34 PM	4:53 PM	9:20 PM
July 5	5:17 AM	5:54 AM	7:01 AM	4:51 AM	8:22 PM	8:33 PM	4:57 PM	9:17 PM
15	5:24 AM	6:00 AM	6:59 AM	5:01 AM	8:17 PM	8:30 PM	5:03 PM	9:10 PM
25	5:33 AM	6:08 AM	6:54 AM	5:14 AM	8:10 PM	8:23 PM	5:09 PM	8:58 PM
Aug 5	5:44 AM	6:17 AM	6:45 AM	5:31 AM	7:58 PM	8:13 PM	5:17 PM	8:41 PM
15	5:54 AM	6:26 AM	6:35 AM	5:46 AM	7:44 PM	8:01 PM	5:24 PM	8:22 PM
25	6:05 AM	6:34 AM	6:24 AM	6:02 AM	7:29 PM	7:48 PM	5:31 PM	8:01 PM
Sept 5	6:16 AM	6:44 AM	6:10 AM	6:19 AM	7:11 PM	7:31 PM	5:38 PM	7:37 PM
15	6:26 AM	6:52 AM	5:56 AM	6:35 AM	6:54 PM	7:16 PM	5:45 PM	7:14 PM
25	6:36 AM	7:00 AM	5:42 AM	6:51 AM	6:37 PM	7:01 PM	5:52 PM	6:51 PM
Oct 5	6:47 AM	7:09 AM	6:28 AM	7:08 AM	6:19 PM	6:45 PM	6:59 PM	6:28 PM
15	6:58 AM	7:18 AM	6:15 AM	7:24 AM	6:03 PM	6:31 PM	7:06 PM	6:07 PM
25	7:10 AM	7:28 AM	6:03 AM	7:41 AM	5:48 PM	6:18 PM	7:15 PM	5:46 PM
Nov 5	6:23 AM	6:40 AM	5:52 AM	7:01 AM	4:34 PM	5:06 PM	7:25 PM	4:26 PM
15	6:35 AM	6:50 AM	5:45 AM	7:18 AM	4:24 PM	4:57 PM	7:34 PM	4:10 PM
25	6:47 AM	7:01 AM	5:40 AM	7:35 AM	4:17 PM	4:51 PM	7:44 PM	3:59 PM
Dec 5	6:58 AM	7:10 AM	5:38 AM	7:49 AM	4:14 PM	4:49 PM	7:53 PM	3:52 PM
15	7:06 AM	7:18 AM	5:39 AM	8:00 AM	4:14 PM	4:51 PM	8:00 PM	3:50 PM
25	7:12 AM	7:23 AM	5:43 AM	8:05 AM	4:19 PM	4:55 PM	8:05 PM	3:54 PM

Prov=Providence; SF=San Francisco; Syd=Sydney; Lon=London
Times are presented in the standard time of the geographical location, using the current time zone of that place.

Window on the Weather

Some relief from severe drought conditions that impacted all three of the Northern Hemisphere's major agriculture growing regions in North America, central Europe and northeast China can be expected this Spring and Summer. Globally, food poverty will ease some and energy strains from severe winter cold will bring further relief to families.

The Sun is entering the fourth year of solar cycle 25 which favors a transition from arid La Niña conditions to a rain producing El Niño ENSO event. Historically, such times are related to early planting seasons during Spring and extended harvest after the Fall Equinox. Additionally, increased atmospheric water vapor will produce milder nighttime temperatures during winter, easing energy bills somewhat even as snowfall across northern regions increases.

The risk from fall hurricanes also diminishes both in the Atlantic basin and western Pacific Ocean, after intense activity in recent years. Conversely, winter storms are likely to be more intense—especially near Full Moons—with the same forces that produce exceptionally high ocean tides intensifying such cycles.

SPRING

MARCH 2023. The emergence of a Pacific Ocean born El Niño event will bring widespread rainfall to key agricultural regions from the Carolinas west to Texas as the Equinox approaches. Several tornado outbreaks are likely, with the greatest risk to Alabama, Georgia and Florida. Nighttime outbreaks of severe weather are more common during late Winter and early Spring. Farther north, late Winter snow is a greater probability than usual from Washington D.C. to Boston. Southern California enjoys further drought relief with above normal rainfall while heavy snow falls in the mountains. Coastal flooding is likely along with high winds that extend northward along the entire West Coast about three times this month. The Great Lakes and northern Plains enjoy mild and dry weather.

APRIL 2023. The promise of a fine growing season begins with widespread rainfall from the southern plains including Texas eastward to Georgia. The Spring wheat crop is markedly improved year over year and portends improvement elsewhere as the season advances. Temperatures are mild coast to coast as arctic air retreats poleward. Storm energy remains present with several severe weather outbreaks brining tornadoes to Kansas, Oklahoma and Texas. New England and the Ohio Valley receive above normal rainfall with mild days and cool nights. While southern California enjoys sunny and mild Spring weather, rainfall persists farther north from San Francisco northward to Seattle. Mountain rains continue , bringing further drought relief and reduced fire risk.

MAY 2023. Generally pleasant Spring weather covers much of the nation this month. Mild days and cool nights prevail from Denver to the East Coast. Flooding rains begin the month near the Gulf Coast to north Florida. Welcome rainfall across the northern Plains brings hope for a broad spectrum of crops through the central and northern Plains. Still, risks for severe thunderstorm outbreaks with isolated tornadoes remain from the Mississippi Valley to Georgia, a natural occurrence during years with El Niño ENSO events. A wet weather Spring weather pattern eases across the Northeast with sunny and mild weather prevailing. California enjoys sunny and seasonable weather with daily coastal fog lingering until midday.

SUMMER

JUNE 2023. Clusters of thunderstorms will migrate across the northern Plains and Great Lakes and on occasion reach New England. Elsewhere, Summer warmth will arrive in time for the solstice. Nighttime temperatures will remain muggy from the Mid-Atlantic states to Florida, where afternoon thunderstorm activity increases on both coasts. Such conditions are also prevalent on the Texas coast. The monsoon season arrives through the intermountain West with lightning visible north of Phoenix and extending north to Idaho. California enjoys splendid early Summer weather with warm days and cool nights. Afternoon sea breezes are gentle along the coast.

JULY 2023. El Niño related conditions regulate temperatures below long-term averages in most places. Along the East Coast, nighttime temperatures will average several degrees above normal. Through the southern Appalachians, late afternoon thunderstorms are a nearly daily event. Such storms are particularly intense along Florida's west coast. New England and the Great Lakes states enjoy frequent breaks from Summer heat along with cold fronts producing gusty showers. Dry weather covers much of the northern Plains and extends through the Pacific Northwest. Frequent thunderstorms continue through western mountain ranges, while valleys turn hot and dry.

AUGUST 2023. In general, agriculture within the United States will recover from near crisis conditions last year to abundance this Summer and Fall. In particular, corn and wheat yields will see marked year over year improvement. The current position within solar cycle 25 supports warm and humid conditions through much of the South with drenching rains through southern states and welcome rainfall bringing near ideal growing conditions from the Ohio Valley westward through the Great Plains. New England enjoys warm days and somewhat muggy nights, though cool Canadian air brings relief on occasion. Florida is keeping a watchful eye for early season tropical storm activity which can develop quickly in the Gulf of Mexico and the Bahamas. The West coast enjoys continued sunny and seasonable weather.

AUTUMN

SEPTEMBER 2023. This year's hurricane activity promises to be somewhat subdued compared to recent years and El Niño replaces La Niña ENSO conditions. Such events limit tropical storm and hurricane development as mid latitude westerly winds' origination across the Pacific Ocean reaches the tropics and prone regions of the Atlantic basin where such storm originate. That same airflow brings occasional rain at higher elevations through the southwest U.S., advancing east and bringing above normal wet weather as far east as the Carolinas. An early season chill arrives in the Pacific Northwest and northern Rockies and some showers keep the forest fire threat quelled. Seasonable weather stretches from the Great Lakes to New England. Florida receives frequent showers and thunderstorms as several tropical easterly waves cross the state.

OCTOBER 2023. Hurricane activity quickly ends across the Atlantic Ocean and in general the weather turns warm and dry across Florida and the Gulf Coast. The Fall harvest arrives with an abundance of crops and the risk for an early frost limited to northern Idaho and eastern Washington state. Fire risk increases some in southern California, while somewhat above normal rainfall persists across the Heartland. Hallomas brings mild and dry weather for much of the country, though coastal showers are likely in Texas. Hot weather is confined to Arizona and the desert Southwest while the Rockies receive the first dusting of snow by the 31st. Thunderstorms bring isolated tornadoes to the central Plains.

NOVEMBER 2023. Mild early Fall weather can be expected across the country through mid-month. Wet weather returns to southern states with the most persistent rainfall from east Texas to Georgia. First frosts arrive across Montana, the Dakotas and northern Minnesota by the 12th. An early snowfall brings several feet of snow to California's Sierra Nevada with accompanying gusty coastal winds as a Pacific storm arrives. Later the same storm brings strong thunderstorms to the southeast U.S. and early season wet snow to the northern Great Lakes states. Windswept rains end the storm along the East Coast followed by ten days of windy and chilly Fall weather for the eastern half of the country.

WINTER

DECEMBER 2023. During weak El Niño ENSO occurrences, weather patterns tend to persist longer with fewer extremes. This month daily temperatures are likely to be normal during the day and slightly above at night. Early Winter snowfall occurs from the Rockies to Chicago. Cleveland and Buffalo receive lake effect snows along with strong winds and arctic cold. New England receives its first snowfall around the 20th. Mild weather persists through southern states, with a brief encounter with severe thunderstorms in Florida.

Stormy weather brings more drought relief to southern California, as heavy snow falls in the mountains. Gale-force winds sweep the Pacific Northwest. Far above normal snowfall blankets Idaho, Montana and the Dakotas with arctic air and strong winds following. Cold and dry weather covers Texas and the rest of the southern Plains.

JANUARY 2024. The risk for excessive snowfall is high this month from Chicago east to New England and as far south as Washington D.C. Major snowfall occurrences are most prevalent during weak to moderate El Niño ENSO events such as has been occurring and also during weak La Niñas. Most occur after January 15, with below normal temperatures preceding a cluster of storms that will occur this year. Western states emerge from stormy weather and enjoy sunny and somewhat milder weather. The immediate West Coast still receives wet weather with high winds and local flooding. Florida also receives wet weather with occasional thunder likely beginning at mid-month. Persistent severe cold covers the northern Plains and Great Lakes states.

FEBRUARY 2024. Stormy Winter weather continues through mid-February with heavy snow and cold culminating with a major East Coast storm ending the series of storms. In some places, single-storm snowfall records are possible as above normal seasonal snowfall levels are reached from New England westward to the Ohio Valley. The risk for heavy snow exists as far south as Virginia and North Carolina. Farther south the risk for nighttime severe weather including tornadoes is high in Georgia and Florida. Flooding rains are also possible. Cool and wet weather also covers Gulf Coast states, including Texas where the risk for an early month ice storm is high. California receives above normal rainfall and strong winds on occasion.

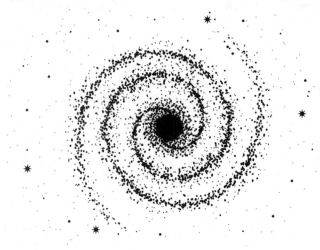

the fixed stars

The Fifteen Behenian Stars

and celestial magic

THERE IS A Native American legend that the stars are really openings in heaven through which our departed loved ones gaze upon those left behind with love. This charming and heartwarming thought reflects many more elaborate beliefs and practices that some stars are actual portals of energy which both generate and attract celestial powers. Rituals which employ crystals and gemstones, plants, kabbalistic words and other sacred symbols known as sigils are meant to attract a given star's influences for healing, love, prosperity or other needs.

There are a number of texts which address this idea, the most well-known of which is Heinrich Cornelius Agrippa's *Three Books of Occult Philosophy*, first

published about 1531. These books were attributed to Hermes Trismegistus, a legendary figure who wrote *Hermetica*, a series of texts which laid the foundation for a variety of magical philosophies. Hermes Trismegistus is associated with the Greek God Hermes, the Roman Mercury and the Egyptian Thoth. According to the prominent British Egyptologist Sir Wallis Budge, a source in Sumeria is most likely for these sacred writings.

Medieval astrologer-magicians from Europe and the Arabian countries employed a select fifteen stars called The Behenian Stars for magical purposes. The name comes from the Arabic word *bahman*, which means "root." When a transiting planet or luminary was within an orb of 6 degrees, the impact of these influential stars was thought to be especially potent. The celestial body's power would combine with that of the star to create a special impact, a vortex of power.

The Royal Stars

Four of the fifteen Behenian stars are in a class by themselves. They are called the Four Royal Stars. Astrologers in ancient Persia believed that the Royal Stars each governed a quarter of the sky—one of the four directions. These four stars were believed to wield incredible potentials for both good and evil. The Four Royal Stars additionally each relate to a specific challenge that an aspirant must overcome in order to become an adept.

Calculations for navigation and calendars were made by referring to all of the Behenian Stars. Future forecasts and predictions and solar as well as lunar cycles were determined by these highly visible stars. Many astrologers today will consider the Behenian stars as well as other fixed stars when interpreting an individual's horoscope or in forecasting the weather and significant world events.

The Four Royal Stars are as follows: Fomalhaut, Antares, Aldebaran and Regulus.

Fomalhaut—also called The Lonely One—is the lone brightest star appearing to be a Fish (*Pisces*) drinking the waters of the Water Bearer (*Aquarius*.) Three thousand years ago it marked the Winter Solstice and so became The Watcher of the South. It is thought to be of sublime scope. Fortunate, powerful and even immortal, it changes from a material to a spiritual focus and great and lasting honors when favorably activated.

Antares is the Watcher of the West. Its origin is Greek and means a rival of Mars. Inhabiting the heart of the Scorpion (*Scorpio*,) this is a bringer of the darkness, the Winter to come. A sinister red super giant star, Antares has an otherworldly aura. In ancient Persia it marked the Autumnal Equinox. Warlike and malefic, headstrong and ravenous, it was related to difficulties and casualties.

Aldebaran is the bright, rose-colored Eye of the Bull in Taurus. It was thought to be a most fortunate star and was The Watcher of the East, marking the Vernal Equinox some three thousand years ago for the astrologers of ancient Persia. Intelligent and eloquent, this star confers courage and popularity. Gain and wealth come through the favor of associates. However, its benefits might not always be long lasting.

Regulus has a name which means "Little King." It is an alpha star of Leo, the Lion. It has special importance because its appearance would foreshadow the rising of Sirius and the start of a New Year for the ancient Egyptians. White and ultramarine blue, this star is the Watcher of the North, marking the Summer Solstice three thousand years ago. Lofty ideals, a royal and magnanimous spirit, ambition, great status and independence are its keynotes.

Behenian Stars in magical rites

Below is a chart of the metaphysical and astrological correlations related to all fifteen Behenian Stars for easy reference, from a 1531 edition of *Three Books of Occult Philosophy* by Heinrich Cornelius Agrippa. The information is attributed to Hermes Trisgmegistus. Other correlations do exist but these are the most consistent and effective for use in connection with magical workings.

To perform a successful ritual in calling upon the energies of the desired fixed star, timing is of the utmost importance. Consider the day of the week and planetary hour as well as the current transits of the luminaries (Sun and Moon) and planets ruling the star. Focusing on the intent of the ritual while drawing the appropriate sigil or kabbalistic words should be part of attracting the desired results. The ruling plants and gemstones can be incorporated into the rite, perhaps placed on an altar or in the center of a cast circle.

Note: the fixed stars actually do move, albeit very slowly. The positions given below were published in the year 2000. They drift at the rate of just one degree every 72 years.

—DIKKI-JO MULLEN

Name	Astrological Location	Planetary Affinity	Gemstone	Plant
Algol	28 Taurus 10	Saturn & Jupiter	Diamond	Black Hellebore
Pleiades	29 Taurus 58	Moon & Mars	Quartz	Fennel
Aldebaran	9 Gemini 47	Mars & Venus	Ruby	Milk Thistle
Capella	21 Gemini 51	Jupiter & Saturn	Sapphire	Thyme
Sirius	14 Cancer 05	Venus	Beryl	Juniper
Procyon	25 Cancer 05	Mercury & Mars	Agate	Buttercup
Regulus	29 Leo 50	Jupiter & Mars	Granite	Mugwort
Polaris	28 Gemini 34	Venus & Moon	Magnet	Succory
Algorab	13 Libra 27	Saturn & Mars	Onyx	Burdock
Spica	23 Libra 50	Venus & Mercury	Emerald	Sage
Arcturus	24 Libra 14	Mars & Jupiter	Jasper	Plantain
Alphecca	12 Scorpio 18	Venus & Mars	Topaz	Rosemary
Antares	9 Sagittarius 46	Venus & Jupiter	Sardonyx	Birthwort
Vega	15 Capricorn 19	Mercury & Venus	Chrysolite	Winter Savory
Deneb Algedi	23 Aquarius 30	Saturn & Mercury	Chalcedony	Marjoram
Fomalhaut	3 Pisces 52	Venus & Mercury	Aquamarine	Poppy

The Magic of the Quadripoint and the Vanishing of the Anasazi

TRAVELING to a destination where it is possible to visit four different places at the same time is an alluring prospect. Since 1931 when the Four Corners Monument opened, it has attracted crowds of visitors of all ages from all parts of the world. The Four Corners monument is a circle divided into four equal, pie-shaped segments with a dot in the middle. Extending from that center dot, a quadripoint, each quarter of the circle touches a different state. It's the only place in the United States where this is possible. In an empty and remote stretch of desert, Utah, Colorado, Arizona and New Mexico intersect. Visitors like to make a photo op as they stand, stretch

and bend to place a limb in each of the four areas marking each state. Many will even be tempted to run around the circle, traveling through all four states in less than a minute.

There is a mystery surrounding the Four Corners which is far deeper than the novelty of visiting the quadripoint, though. The mystery is thousands of years old—there are records of it left in stone and in the oral traditions of the Hopi, Zuni and Navajo today. These are reminders of the Anasazi, other people who lived in another time. Anasazi: the name derives from a Navajo word which means "ancient enemies." The Anasazi lived in the region of what is now the Four Corners area for well over a thousand years. Then within a single generation between 1275 and 1300 CE they all suddenly disappeared. Some long-forgotten tragedy, an unknown catastrophic event, forced them to suddenly abandon their homes and flee.

The story of the Anasazi began, according to archeologists, about 35 hundred years ago. A sophisticated civilization arose in what is now a barren desert. It rivaled and perhaps even surpassed those of the ancient Egyptians, the Aztec and the Maya. It all began when hunter gatherers began to cultivate the three sisters, named for the three important crops: beans, corn and squash. Gradually the people realized that they had to stay in one place to nurture the fields of food and they began to establish permanent homes.

These mysterious and intelligent people discovered the golden ratio used by builders in Egypt in the architecture of the pyramids and temples and constructed elaborate multistory works of masonry. One in Chaco Canyon had over 800 rooms. In the 1880s, when these ruins were first discovered by visitors from the East coast, the buildings were larger than multifamily residences being erected in New York City!

There were enclosures which might have been built to keep animals and also meeting areas with seating to accommodate many. They carved dwellings into ledges high above the desert floor which included kitchens, windows and more details that suggest a wealthy and comfortable lifestyle. Preserved by the dry climate, modern archeologists have found various possessions abandoned by the Anasazi. Weaving and sewing tools with remnants of cloth fashioned from cotton and yucca fibers, sandals, clothing as well as beautifully decorated pottery and furniture were all among the discoveries.

The Anasazi built observatories which hint at how important cosmology was to them. A petroglyph drawing was found recording a supernova which modern astronomers believe exploded in the sky in 1054 CE. Perhaps this was seen as an omen and created a panic which resulted in the sudden abandonment.

Chaco Canyon, preserved as a National Park in northeastern New Mexico, offers the best evidence of how elaborate the Anasazi culture really was. It seems to have been a

be the descendants of the Anasazi. Understandably this is perceived as insulting. Other investigations point to increasing incidents of civil unrest. Abandoned weapons suggest that violence was perpetrated against those who perished as victims of crimes. One of the ancestor stories repeated by Native Americans today involves terrorism brought by bands of thugs who invaded from further South. This might have forced the remaining Anasazi to flee to the Northeast to hide in the Mesa Verde area in Colorado.

A visit to Chaco Canyon and the Four Quarters area is memorable and magical. At night, far from the ambient light of any cities, the sky offers dramatic views of starry vistas. Walking near the remains of the cliff dwellings suggests spectral presences. Even deeper mysteries can come to mind. The Navajo of today are not fond of visiting the Anasazi sites. The feeling is that the abandoned cities are the sacred abodes of spirits who are best left alone.

The Four Corners Monument is managed by the Navajo Nation. It is open daily from 8:00 am until 4:45 pm. There are picnic tables, but no running water, electricity or other services. Bring cash to pay for admission, as the nearest ATM is probably located 65 miles away in Bluff, Utah. Bring your own water. There is a phone—the number is 928-206-2540. Authentic Native American jewelry and other handicrafts are offered for sale. The site is located 6 miles North of Teec Nos Pos, Arizona on State Hwy 597.

—ESTHER NEUMEIER

regional trade center, a great city with paved roads leading to and from the many small pueblos or villages. The remains of these still dot the region today. Wooden beams used in the buildings might offer a clue about the fate of the lost civilization: tree rings in the logs show evidence of climate change. The patterns in the rings showed years of decreasing rainfall which could have led to mass starvation because of crop failures. Skeletal remains seem to tell a more sinister story. Archeologists have found indications of cannibalism. This theory is angrily refuted by the indigenous tribes of today who might

THE WITCHES' RUNES—THE STONES O'LEARY

Stones O'Leary,
Stones O'Leary,
Tell me truly,
Tell me clearly.
Give to me an answer true,
Show me what I am to do.
Let my eye see clear and bright,
That I may keep my future right.

CONSISTING OF TEN marked stones, this divinatory system first appears in the writings of psychic and occultist Dolores Ashcroft-Nowicki in the 20th century. Writing in *Quadriga* magazine, a periodical circulated mostly amongst students of English ritual magician Gareth Knight, Ashcroft-Nowicki wrote about a system of fortune telling using "gypsy" stones—the Stones O'Leary—in 1977. They have since appeared in the published work and private materials of authors and Witches such as Patricia Crowther, Simon Goodman, Marian Green and others.

The stones' imagery—an eye, birds in flight, two crossed spears, the Sun, the Moon, a star, three rings, a sickle, water and grain—is simple enough that readings are fairly easy to perform, however their meanings are complex and provide layered meaning and a deeper look at things, especially when in certain combinations.

It's generally recommended that you make your own set of stones O'Leary from stones you find yourself. In the original 1977 article, Ashcroft-Nowicki advised readers to take their time with this process.

Reading the Witches' runes

Readings are performed by placing the Eye stone face up and holding the other nine stones in both hands. The reader then blows on the stones and casts or drops them onto and around the Eye stone. Any stones that lie face down are discarded and the remaining stones are interpreted in a spiral pattern, reading outwards from the Eye stone.

The Eye: represents the querent, the signifier. Place face up at the start

of a reading. Australian Witch Simon Goodman proposed that it was related in some way to the God Odin.

The Birds: messages, unexpected news, communication, children, journeys and travel. Adjacent to the Moon stone, the Birds can sometime signal a sudden and serious illness.

The Crossed Spears: conflict, discord, unrest, clashing energies and heated parting words. Alongside the Sickle, this is a serious argument or falling out.

The Moon: clouded vision, something hidden or not yet come into awareness, dreams, the Otherworld and intuition. Dolores Ashcroft-Nowicki related this stone to feminine energy and to the querent's personality.

The Rings: a bonding or partnership, a link between two situations or people, a binding. Patricia Crowther surmised that the combination of the Rings and the Waves pointed to a romance that will take the querent abroad.

The Sickle: death, monumental change, an abrupt and drastic ending. When present near the Waves, it often points to a physical parting such as someone moving away.

The Star: ambitions, ideals, energy, inspiration, hope, seeing clearly. When the Sun and the Star land near each other they represent the querent's hopes and dreams, but these hopes and dreams will go unfulfilled if the Moon is present without the Sun.

The Sun: strength, growth, positive aspects, energy and fruitfulness. Patricia Crowther claimed that having the Sun as the "leading" stone in a reading— that is having it the closest stone to the Eye—was a sign of a successful

year ahead. When it appears nearby the Wheat, the Sun usually signals the birth of something new.

The Water/The Waves: high emotions, fluid situations, the Underworld. Alongside the Moon, this stone sometimes points to an accident or illness. The Waves with the Star is often the birth of a child in or around the querent's family.

The Wheat/The Ripe Grain: harvest, profit, the rewards of hard work— especially physical work, endings and climaxes. Simon Goodman wrote that the combination of the Wheat and the Rings often speak to a business partnership. If the Rings and the Wheat are present in a reading with three or more other stones other than the main Eye stone, it is often a sign that the entire reading is for the querent's family rather than the querent.

—JOSEPHINE WINTER

With thanks to Ryan McLeod and his thorough research into this oft-overlooked but nevertheless wonderful system.

Corinna's going a Maying

Get up, get up for shame, the Blooming Morne
Upon her wings presents the god unshorne.
 See how *Aurora* throwes her faire
 Fresh-quilted colours through the aire:
 Get up, sweet-Slug-a-bed, and see
 The Dew-bespangling Herbe and Tree.
Each Flower has wept, and bow'd toward the East,
Above an houre since; yet you not drest,
 Nay! not so much as out of bed?
 When all the Birds have Mattens seyd,
 And sung their thankful Hymnes: 'tis sin,
 Nay, profanation to keep in,
When as a thousand Virgins on this day,
Spring, sooner than the Lark, to fetch in May.

Rise; and put on your Foliage, and be seene
To come forth, like the Spring-time, fresh and greene;
 And sweet as *Flora*. Take no care
 For Jewels for your Gowne, or Haire:
 Feare not; the leaves will strew
 Gemms in abundance upon you:
Besides, the childhood of the Day has kept,
Against you come, some *Orient Pearls* unwept:
 Come, and receive them while the light
 Hangs on the Dew-locks of the night:
 And *Titan* on the Eastern hill
 Retires himselfe, or else stands still
Till you come forth. Wash, dresse, be briefe in praying:
Few Beads are best, when once we goe a Maying.

Come, my *Corinna*, come; and comming, marke
How each field turns a street; each street a Parke
 Made green, and trimm'd with trees: see how
 Devotion gives each House a Bough,
 Or Branch: Each Porch, each doore, ere this,
 An Arke a Tabernacle is
Made up of white-thorn neatly enterwove;
As if here were those cooler shades of love.

Can such delights be in the street,
And open fields, and we not see't?
Come, we'll abroad; and let's obay
The Proclamation made for May:
And sin no more, as we have done, by staying;
But my *Corinna*, come, let's goe a Maying.

There's not a budding Boy, or Girle, this day,
But is got up, and gone to bring in May.
A deale of Youth, ere this, is come
Back, and with *White-thorn* laden home.
Some have dispatcht their Cakes and Creame,
Before that we have left to dreame:
And some have wept, and woo'd, and plighted Troth,
And chose their Priest, ere we can cast off sloth:
Many a green-gown has been given;
Many a kisse, both odde and even:
Many a glance too has been sent
From out the eye, Loves Firmament:
Many a jest told of the Keyes betraying
This night, and Locks pickt, yet w'are not a Maying.

Come, let us goe, while we are in our prime;
And take the harmlesse follie of the time.
We shall grow old apace, and die
Before we know our liberty.
Our life is short; and our dayes run
As fast away as do's the Sunne:
And as a vapour, or a drop of raine
Once lost, can ne'r be found againe:
So when or you or I are made
A fable, song, or fleeting shade;
All love, all liking, all delight
Lies drown'd with us in endlesse night.
Then while time serves, and we are but decaying;
Come, my *Corinna*, come, let's goe a Maying.

—ROBERT HERRICK

Robert Herrick was a 17th-century English lyric poet and cleric. He is best known for Hesperides, *a book of poems.*

The Witch Saints of Stregoneria

STREGONERIA is the path of Italian sorcery, an umbrella term covering popular superstition, secular folk magic and survivals—or revivals—of pre-Christian esoteric traditions. Like many still-living strains of sorcery, practitioners of Stregoneria often maintain dual faith allegiance.

Patrons of Witchcraft

There are several saints who have emerged as the matrons and patron saints of Witchcraft, mediumship and sorcery. Such saints as these are acknowledged as "Witch-saints," or are likened to elves and goblins. A few of these saints fall neatly into categories of Pagan god masquerading as Christian spirit or hidden heretic in the holy kingdom. Others straddle multiple worlds and refuse to be pigeonholed.

Those saints masking Pagan deities are perhaps the most understandable for those outside looking in. This is also the most alluring for newcomers eager to discard the Catholic cultural trappings, who want to return to the wholesale veneration of

pre-Christian deities, no questions asked. Sadly, they often discard the most valuable parts of the Italian cultural matrix with the saints. Additionally, opinions vary—region to region, town to town, family to family—as to which saint masks which deity, or if masking is happening at all.

In southern Italian and Italian-American Stregoneria, the most popular spiritual mother of the *maghi* (magical practitioners) is either Our Lady of Tindari or Our Lady of Mount Carmel, the latter especially in her warrior aspects. The most popular spiritual patron of the maghi is Saint Michael the Archangel.

Tindari's church is built on a temple to Cybele which itself stood upon a shrine to Tanith. Mount Carmel may mask Isis, Diana or Ceres, depending on the region of Italy. Michael the Archangel is linked with Apollo, Soranus, Lucifer and Dis Pater. However, most current practitioners are fiercely loyal to them as Tindari, Mount Carmel, and Michael.

Another example of this type of Witch-saint lies in the cult of Saint Lucy. In life Lucia was renowned for her piety and devotion. She rejected suitors—including her own father—and tore out her eyes in defiance. As a saint Lucy is also associated with the breaking of *il malocchio* (the evil eye,) the seeing of truth and gaining victory in spiritual warfare. Her church in Syracuse, Sicily is built over the temple of Diana Lucifera, though some identify her with Iuno Lucina. Some streghe teach that she allows them to continue the worship of one or both of these Goddesses. It must be stressed again that these links between old Gods and Christian saints are nuanced and many older practitioners may balk (at least publicly) at the merest suggestion that their beloved saint may hide an ancient God or Goddess under their robes.

Magical co-conspirators

Other saints are cultivated as co-conspirators and fellow practitioners of the art magical. Some of these maintain double hagiographies—one the epitome of orthodox sanctity, the other riddled with hints that they were more than a mere Christian lamb. The Catholic devout approach these saints through proper means whereas streghe conjure them for true dreams, spiritual mentorship and direct aid.

Saint Cyprian of Carthage with his beloved Justina are examples of such Saints. Saint Cyprian—who is growing in popularity within the greater magical community—is said to have never given up the practice of the art magical.

Saint Anthony of Padua is another example of these faith-straddling spirits. In Tuscany he may be petitioned at a home or church altar like a proper saint or in a cellar like a folletti—a Pagan deity demoted to elven status. Many Sicilian streghe identify him with Hermes, especially in his aspects as road-opener, wonder-worker and silver-tongued muse. In folk magic, Saint Anthony is frequently called upon to find lost objects—lost lovers, lost items, stolen property and lost power.

Witch-saints are bridges between the status quo and the clandestine, the orthodox and the occult. For those who cultivate them as allies, they are fierce protectors and liaisons between the worlds.

—JONATHAN SOUSA

Recommended Reading

Encyclopedia of Mystics, Saints, and Sages by Judika Iles
By-Paths in Sicily by Eliza Osborn Heaton
Etruscan Roman Remains by Charles G. Leland

Mysterious Green Earth Children from a Subterranean Country

HISTORICAL RECORDS of the time state that a brother and sister emerged from underground during the reign of King Stephen of England (between 1135–1154.) It was during the autumn harvest when the mystery began in the village of Woolpit in Suffolk. The name Woolpit derives from an early Anglo-Saxon word, *wulff-pytt*. The reference is to the deep trenches or pits which were once dug to trap wolves. Something else seems to be needed as well, something that has hardly been discussed by any of the above-mentioned scholars and magicians. There was, however, one person who may have figured out what that something else might be, some five and a half centuries ago.

It was from out of one of these very deep and dark holes that two children climbed. Their clothes were described as strange and, even stranger, their skin was a green color. They seemed confused as they wandered into the field toward the workers and stood watching the reaping. Finally the laborers grew concerned and took the youngsters—who appeared to

be about eight to ten years old—into the village to be questioned. No one could understand the language they spoke although they conversed with each other.

Eventually the young strangers were taken to the household of an important person, a landholder named Richard de Calne. They became hysterical and refused to eat the food offered. This continued for days and it seemed as if the children would starve. Then they saw some bean stalks. They became very excited and motioned that they wanted the green beans. When they tore the stalks open and found them hollow both of them burst into tears. Someone showed them how to take the beans off the stalks and, desperate for food, they ate. Over time they began to nibble bread. The boy—the younger and smaller of the two—didn't thrive. Eventually he weakened and died but the girl fared better. She adjusted to her new home, attended church and was baptized. The greenish tinge to her skin faded and she became healthy and beautiful.

The girl learned English and was able to recall her early childhood. She said that the children were a brother and sister and that their home was in a world of perpetual twilight. All of those who lived there were green and the place was named Saint Martin. She could not say where this was located, but there was a great river across which a luminous land could be seen in the distance. One day, the girl said, she and her little brother were watching her father's cattle. They followed the animals into a cavern and there were distant sounds of bells. Later she would say they were church bells. The children wandered into the dark cavern further and further and became lost and frightened. They emerged as if from the mouth of a cave into the bright, blinding sunlight. This was brighter than any light they had ever seen before. They were terrified by the farm workers and tried to return to find the entrance back to the cave, but could not. That's when they were observed, caught and taken to the village.

The girl took the name Agnes Barre. As is often true of the faerie folk, she acquired a reputation for promiscuous, wild and wanton behavior. She married well, though, to an ambassador of King Henry ll. Today the current Earl Ferrers, Robert Shirley, the 14th Earl, claims to be descended from this union.

There are several versions of this legend of the green children, seemingly orphans, from a subterranean civilization, but this is the most consistent. A supernatural link to another dimension has been suggested. One account of the green children is as recent as 1828. Other studies are even more contemporary, as recent as 1965 and 1998. Some relegate it all to the realm of imagination, a mere fairy story. Green is a color long thought to be magical and sacred to the wee folk. The legends of Jack in the Green, the Green Man of the forest and the Arthurian account of Sir Gawain and the Green Knight in Camelot all support this idea.

The Scottish astronomer Duncan Lunan suggests that the children were aliens, transported from another planet. Two credible historians from the time of King Stephen, Ralph of Coggeshall and William of Newburgh, wrote extensively about the green children. Coggeshall mentions them in his *Chronicon Anglicanum*, saying he frequently spoke about them with Richard de Calne. In his *Historia Rerum Anglicarum*, Newburgh cites "many competent witnesses" who had seen the boy and girl.

Skeptics scoff and say the children were probably speaking Flemish, which would have been a strange language to those in Suffolk, and that they wandered from Fornham St. Martin and the water was the River Lark. This doesn't make sense though, because the Flemish mercenaries had already been expelled from England and the distance was too far for small children to have wandered. Also the River Lark was too narrow to seem like a vast waterway. To this day, after nearly a thousand years the mystery and speculation continue.

—GRANIA LING

To Marry the Cosmos

(Notes Toward a General Theory of Magic, Part 7)

ALL THE SCHOLARS on whose work we have drawn in the previous six of these Notes—philosophers, philologists, linguists, anthropologists, folkorists, historians of magic and working magicians—have treated magic as a sort of art or craft or technology, as if it were a simple matter of cause and effect: if you understand the causes and principles of magic well enough, you can produce magical effects on demand, in accordance with your will alone. And yet... magic is rarely quite that easy in actual practice. Something else seems to be needed as well, something that has hardly been discussed by any of the above-mentioned scholars and magicians. There was, however, one person who may have figured out what that something else might be, some five and a half centuries ago.

To Work Magic is to Marry the Cosmos

In the late 1400s a brash and brilliant young genius flashed forth briefly in the firmament of the brightest stars of the Renaissance in Italy. His name was Giovanni Pico della Mirandola, and he was murdered when he was just 31 years old, poisoned by men who found his brilliance, his scholarship and his passion for Truth at any cost far too subversive of the established verities of science and religion (such as they were then.)

IOANNES PICVS PR MIRAND.

It was late in 1486—when he was only 23 years old—that Pico published a very short book in Latin titled *Nine Hundred Conclusions in Every Kind of Knowledge*. In it he concisely stated 900 theses, ranging over all the branches of knowledge. He also announced that he would defend all these 900 theses in public debates at Rome during the following year. Every one of his 900 theses represented a challenge to one or another point of learning and doctrine that churchmen and professors had long regarded as settled and would have preferred to leave unchallenged forever.

Among Pico's 900 theses were very many esoteric ones, including 15 theses on Zoroaster and the Chaldean Oracles, 72 on the Cabala and Christianity, 31 on the Orphic Hymns…and 26 on magic!

Pico, naive and unworldly youth that he was, seems to have expected that his book would be welcomed by all, and that the debate he had announced would be an eagerly anticipated event. What happened instead was that the pope forbade Pico to hold his proposed debates and prohibited his small book from being circulated and read by anyone at all—the first book to be universally prohibited by the Church in over a thousand years. Less than a dozen copies of the first printing of Pico's book are known to have survived this prohibition.

It is Pico's 26 theses on magic that demand our attention here, and in particular the thirteenth of them:

"Magicam operari non est aliud quam maritare mundum."

(To work magic is nothing other than to marry the world.)

By *mundum*, "the world," Pico understands the entire world, the cosmos, not just the world of matter and energy, situated in time and space. But the most surprising part of this thesis is Pico's choice of the verb *maritare*, "to marry."

What Does It Mean to Marry the Cosmos?

A marriage is a union of at least two sentient, living beings. Here the beings in question are two in number, the magician and the cosmos (which in Pico's day was presumed to be both sentient and alive.) Significantly, too, marriage presupposes courtship. If any magician would marry the cosmos, then that magician must first have courted the cosmos and won its consent—and, we may presume, the cosmos has also courted the magician!—before their marriage can be truly solemnized.

Of course, in the strongest of marriages, each partner will continue to court the other long after the marriage ceremony has been completed, throughout the entire duration of their marriage. And as we already saw in the sixth of these Notes, a marriage so strong as that has occult power: it will eventually lead the married partners into the Imaginal realm, the realm where the most powerful magic is worked.

So...Pico appears to be claiming here that magic is not merely a kind of technology or craft that a person might hope to master, but that it requires an ongoing *mutual* courtship of the living, sentient cosmos by a magician, and of the magician by the cosmos. It can never be enough to have mastered all the tools and techniques of the craft of magic. One must court and win magic herself (or himself) as one would court and win a desired lover, if one would attain the highest reaches of the art of magic—which is therefore not a craft or a technology, but an actual art.

This, I think, is the overlooked point in all present-day theorizing about magic and how it works. It seems also to be the chief prerequisite for working the very strongest and wisest magic.

All honor to Pico for his profound insight!

Can There Be a Unified General Theory of All Magic?

The reader of all seven of these Notes may easily suppose that the General Theory of Magic I have been formulat-

ing here is meant to cover the totality of magic. Indeed, it does seem to cover all the kinds of magic that are worked by words and deeds, using myths and rituals. These things are indeed powerful. As Rudyard Kipling remarked in 1923, addressing the Royal College of Surgeons of England, "Words are, of course, the most powerful drug used by mankind." By implication, the same is true of rituals and myths.

However, there is also another, much rarer sort of magic, worked in a wholly other way than by means of words and other symbols, that is excessively difficult to describe. Despite this difficulty, we ought not to end this series of Notes without saying a few words about it.

Scholars who study mysticism draw a useful distinction between *kataphatic* and *apophatic* methods of achieving mystical experiences.

Kataphatic methods are methods of affirmation. Mystics who use these methods build on the evidence of their senses and the power of their thoughts and feelings, to make their way toward the Divine. They try to grasp the Numinous by starting from the most awesome, glorious and holy experiences that people have in ordinary life. On this foundation, using all the powers of words and reason, of deeds and love, of symbols and patterns, of myths and rituals, they draw ever nearer and nearer to their Deities or Numinous Realities.

Apophatic methods, in sharp contrast, assume that all inputs from our bodily senses, all activities of our mind, are mighty obstacles to experiencing Divinity as It truly is, in and of Itself. The apophatic mystic proceeds by systematically tearing down each and every one of these barriers, by denying any validity and utility to every activity of the bodily senses and the embodied mind, to every sort of sensation and mentation. This is a much harder road for a mystic to travel. Few will venture on it, and very few indeed are those who travel it to its end. It is also a much more dangerous road than the kataphatic road— it is beset on all sides with powerful forces of delusion and temptation.

Also, as is the way of the cosmos, sometimes a person will suddenly find himself standing at the end of this road for a time, though he has made no effort to travel it, or even had any suspicion that such a road might exist and might lead to such a goal. Sometimes it is the cosmos itself that will start courting a future mystic or magician of its own volition, for reasons of its own that are usually opaque to the human whom it is courting.

Kataphatic and Apophatic Magic

As with mysticism, so there are kataphatic methods and apophatic methods of working magic.

The sort of magic we have been discussing in these Notes is most definitely kataphatic. So the General Theory of Magic that we have been building is a theory of *kataphatic magic* only. Indeed, as far as most practicing magicians ever know, this is the only sort of magic that there is.

However, *apophatic magic* also exists, though it is rarely practiced and even more rarely talked about. Like apophatic mysticism, apophatic magic is quite difficult and quite dangerous to work, for much the same reasons. Because of these dangers, I will say only a few words about it here, now that I have come to the end of these seven Notes.

We humans are at the mercy not only of our native languages (as pointed out in the sixth of these Notes,) but also at the mercy of our bodies and minds. Our physical senses severely limit our ability to perceive the cosmos in its wholeness, and our physical brain and nervous system further restrict our ability to·grasp what little of the cosmos we have perceived. These limits of ours are "baked in the cake" of being human. As far as most people can ever tell, these are the only two means any human has to experience the Cosmos.

These limitations are not a regrettable feature of human life, but a very valuable one. As a very wise woman once said, "It is our limitations that keep us sane." Were we not so strictly limited by our material existence, we would be eternally lost in a vast ocean of delusion and temptation.

Apophatic magicians, like apophatic mystics, know that there is a way to transcend these limits and to achieve *direct perception* of the Numinous Cosmos, that is, perception which is entirely unmediated by our physical human body. To achieve direct perception, to transcend every bodily limit of sensation and mentation, would-be apophatic magicians will carefully examine, each in its own turn, each and every activity of their physical senses and of the physical brain and nervous system that seems to give them any idea of the "real" world. By challenging and overcoming each of these sensations and mentations in its turn, one comes

to see that it is a mere illusion created by the natural—severe, yet beneficial—limitations of one's human body.

Stripping away one illusion after another, one eventually comes to a sort of blank wall, a dark cloud of unknowing and unsensing. This blank wall, however, is an illusion, too—it is the last illusion of them all. Apply the same process to it and strip it away.

Then, and only then, will one *perceive*—not through any bodily senses and not by any action of the bodily mind, but *directly*—the Numinous Cosmos as it truly is. This is the *direct perception* of all things as they truly are, in all their mutual interconnectedness and unity, the living fiery web of total interconnection that stands wholly outside time and space and is no sort of matter or energy whatever.

This final *direct perception* is indeed wholly independent of the

> *"Pray, read, read, read, re-read,*
> *labor, and you will discover."*

body's sense organs—in no way does it resemble any indirect perceptions that come through these sense organs. It is also wholly independent of the body's brain and nervous system, of its words and thoughts—in no way does it resemble any possible thought or any possible speech.

The only way speech can capture even the smallest hint of the taste of the experience of direct perception is by words that defy both logic and common experience. As the mystic Dionysius the Areopagite wrote in *The Mystical Theology* around 500 CE, in direct perception one "leaves behind everything sensed and understood, everything that *can be* sensed and understood, all that is not and all that is." That is where "the mysteries…lie simple, absolute and unchangeable in the brilliant darkness of a hidden silence. Amid the deepest shadow they pour overwhelming light on what is most manifest. Amid the wholly unsensed and unseen they completely fill our sightless minds with treasures beyond all beauty."

Once you have experienced this direct perception of the entire interconnected, sentient Cosmos as a whole, you no longer need any rituals or any myths—much less any "Laws of Magic"—to work what to most people will seem to be genuine miracles. You merely have to return to direct perception—ah, would that this were so easy to do as it is to say!—and then reach out with a thing that might be called a limb, but is nothing like a bodily limb, and tug ever so gently on one strand or another of that net of living fire that contains all things as its knots and joins them into one vast Wholeness.

But then, too, you will perceive the harm that working such powerful magic, even with the best of human intentions, can very often bring to the people for whose supposed benefit you might propose to work it. This is particularly true when the impulse to work a miracle for another's sake arises in yourself, and is not an impulse from the Cosmos itself.

And that is all, I suppose, that can safely be said about apophatic magic, if indeed it can properly still be called magic and not miracle-working.

At the End of Our Journey Together

Here I end my series of seven "Notes Toward a General Theory of Magic." I hope, dear reader, that you may have found them worth your time. I have wrought them as well as I knew how. Yet they should be taken merely as launching pads for your own thoughts and further work.

As a long-ago alchemist, the author of the *Mutus Liber* (The Mute Book) wrote in 1667, *Ora, lege, lege, lege, relege, labora, et invenies* "Pray, read, read, read, re-read, labor, and you will discover."

—ROBERT MATHIESEN

At the Roof of the World

Divinity on Mount Everest

THE MOUNTAIN that many Westerners see as the ultimate challenge of human endurance and physicality has since time immemorial been the abode of divinity Hindu and Buddhist alike.

At the base of Mount Everest two worlds mingle where secular encounters the divine. The ethnically Tibetan *Sherpas* know Everest as *Chomolungma* (Goddess Mother of Mountains) which is the abode of the divinity, Miyolangsangma, the Goddess of inexhaustible giving.

The Demons of Khumbu

It is said that Miyolangsangma in a time before time was not known as the Goddess of inexhaustible giving. Rather she was known as one of five sister demons that originally inhabited the five Himalayan peaks of the Khumbu region. In time, they would achieve enlightenment, becoming the Buddhist guardians known as the Five Long Life Sisters,

each attaining a virtue. Of course Miyolangsangma attained the virtue of inexhaustible giving.

In the tale of the conversion of the five demon sisters, it is the great Padmasambhava—the lotus born saint known as Guru Rimpoche—who brought the teachings of the Buddha to them. It was from that moment that they vowed to cause no harm and to be the guardians of the mountains as well as those seeking truth.

Upon their taking up the way of the Buddha, the sisters traveled to India to receive the deepest knowledge from the masters Lobpon Chogyi Gocha and Mahasiddha Kanha. It was there that they learned the dark secrets of Charnel Grounds—a land filled with the horror of rotting bodies, wandering ghosts and other terrifying beings—conquering the attachment to the physical, the craving for a future, the fear of death and the fear of impermanence.

In a later time, the five sisters resolved to test the fortitude of the great saint and yogi Milarepa. They sent many disturbing apparitions to upset his meditations. It was said that the unenlightened would have been truly terrified by the phantoms they sent to disturb the yogi. Unwilling to break their oath of harming none, they took it no further. They returned some days later, affirming again that they would protect the Buddhadharma and pronounced their essence in the form of a mantra—which to this day is used to invoke their protection. Miyolangsangma and her sisters would encounter Milarepa twice more to have bestowed upon them the teachings of Enlightenment Thought, Mudra Yoga and Karma Mudra.

Guardians and the Mountain

Miyolangsangma and her sisters have a special connection with the Sherpa, the peoples that inhabit the Khumbu region, an area spanning the base of the five peaks. In turn the Sherpa have a deep connection with the five sisters and have tended to the ritual obligations to Miyolangsangma. They have described the mountain Chomolungma (Mount Everest) as the palace, temple and playground of Miyolangsangma. They assert that they as well as the many visitors who journey there are merely guests in her home.

Everest became the mountain to conquer when it was finally confirmed that is was the tallest peak on this planet. In May 1953, Sir Edmund Hillary was guided to the summit by the Sherpa Tenzing Norgay. Tenzing had good knowledge of Miyolangsangma, being

a longtime devotee of the Goddess. He acted as a guide and guardian for many years, summiting several times. So deep was his connection with Chomolungma that legend has it that Tenzing's second wife was an incarnation of the Goddess Miyolangsangma. His family has continued to guide climbers.

Regardless of faith, it is tradition that, that climbers will seek out the blessings of the lamas before their expedition to the top of the mountain. In fact, many Sherpa will not guide a group without going through the *Puja* (ceremony to honor a deity.) During the ceremony, juniper leaves are burned while prayers are said over the expedition equipment. Traditional food and drink offerings are made with much chanting of the mantra of Miyolangsangma. Finally, the climbers smear their faces with gray tsampa flour, symbolizing their goal to return and see each other in old age.

—DEMETRIUS SANTIAGO

Photo Credit: Sunrise from Burrow Mump, Burrowbridge, Somerset by Ian Herlock

HEAVEN OF EARTH

The Climax of the Descent of Matter

"I love the Earth."

The driver pretended he didn't hear me. From the moment he collected me at the airport in Bristol he allowed me to sit silently and be seduced by the charm and splendor of southwest England's green and pleasant pastures. Radstock, near Bath in Somerset, was my destination. It was an area of the UK I'd never visited before so I had no idea how long I would be able to savor my chauffeured religious experience.

Never had I seen so many shades of green in my life. It felt like I was living inside the swelling phrases of Blake's great national hymn, *Jerusalem*. A "countenance divine" did indeed shine forth upon these clouded hills. This was heaven on Earth. No. This was heaven *of* Earth.

I rolled down the window and inhaled the perfume of grass and soil warmed by the sun of mid-July.

"I love the Earth." I said again, this time under my breath.

I closed my eyes as if to take a snapshot of the moment, and was surprised to feel a tear burst over the lower lash of my right eye and coolly evaporate in the wind as it ran down my cheek. I assure you, in my jaded heart such sensitive moments are a rarity, and usually occur only in the fleeting seconds that follow the first and second sip of a late afternoon martini. (Regrettably, this pure bliss disappears around the third and fourth sip.) This day's rapture was most likely induced by the stress and debauchery of visiting five countries in seven days, and the realization that after this lecture I'd be returning home to my own bed. Whatever the cause, I was drunk on Earth and wished the driver would stop the car so that I might stretch out in a field and soak the verdant ground with my tears of love.

The mental image of such an awkward and unseemly act immediately erased such daydreams, but for the first time in my life I realized deep down to the very core of my soul that the Earth is a living, breathing, conscious being—an intelligence—a God(dess)—and that I was her child. My flesh her soil and mantle; my blood her rivers and streams and seas; my bones her stones and mountains; my heartbeat her molten core—my soul one with her soul.

What more palpable deity could humanity seek? What God more wonderful, more worthy of our awe, our gratitude, our prayers? We must certainly honor the Sun as the ultimate source of light and life, but without Earth to reflect the solar glory, without the Earth and her manifold creatures *Sol Invictus* (the unconquered sun) would remain eternally a God unworshipped.

Moreover, is not the Earth herself sunlight made manifest? Earth is the climax of spirit's descent into matter—the magical lowest low that contains not only a spark of the highest high but everything else in between. Earth is the alchemical laboratory that transmutes light into life. Earth is the crowning finale of creation, and we are conscious creatures of the Earth. As such you and I possess—we embody—the secret of spirit's return to godhead. As it is written in the *Emerald Tablet of Hermes* via Hall's *Lost Keys of Freemasonry*, "That *One Only Thing* (after God) is the father of all things in the universe. Its power is perfect, after it has been united to a spirituous earth."

It is humanity's most ancient and self-evident fact of life—the Sun is our father, the Earth is our mother—and no matter how gender neutral our culture may strive to become, it is the mother who first hears our cries. It is the mother who first responds to our needs. It is the mother who first answers our questions.

How ironic it is, then, that as we grow into headstrong youngsters we become less and less inclined to listen to the voice of our mother. As hormone-blinded adolescents we embarrassedly shun her counsel and ridicule her prophetic warnings regarding the dire consequences of our shortsightedness and foolish behavior. As self-absorbed young adults we shut our minds completely to the possibility she could in any way understand what *our* life is like, or what is or is not in our best interest. It is not until we have reached a significant level of maturity that we realize that we've been blessed since birth with our own personal omniscient oracle, one whose unconditional love for us is beyond all human comprehension.

For centuries the art of Geomancy has been a proper and respectful means by which we, as children of the Earth, purposefully affirm our recognition of the Earth as a living intelligence capable of answering our questions. For Renaissance mystics it was the divinatory method of choice. For those today who feel the heartbeat of the Mother beneath our feet, perhaps it is time we approach the earthen altar and seek her wise counsel.

–LON MILO DUQUETTE

Editor's note: The title of this article is a reference to John Michael Greer's books *The Art and Practice of Geomancy: Divination, Magic, and Earth Wisdom of the Renaissance* and *Allow Me to Introduce—An Insider's Guide to the Occult*.

Y Ddraig Goch a'r
Y Ddraig Wen

The Red Dragon and

the White Dragon

DRAGON'S FIRE has burned in the hearts of the Britons for millennia. This mystical creature has not only been the totem of pre-Saxon Britons, it has also represented the very soul of the Celts that inhabited the isle. In fact, it represents the very connection that the people have with the spirits of the land itself. With the arrival of the Germanic warriors, the island of Britain gained another dragon— the white dragon of the Saxons.

In the two tales below, the dragons are contained in the first and released in the second. Over time the soul of the Britons has become both the red dragon and the white dragon—Cymro (Welshman) and Saxon—and they can indeed live in peace. The red dragon and the white dragon were briefly united in the royal coat of arms of the Tudors.

Lludd and Llevelys and the dragons

To Beli the Great was born four sons, the eldest being Lludd and the youngest being Llevelys. It was into the hands of the eldest that the rulership of the Island of Britain would fall. He ruled compassionately and brought prosperity to the kingdom, fortifying the capital and dominions. None knew hunger nor thirst under the rule of Lludd. In the precincts of the capital, he raised a mighty castle named Caer Lludd which in time became Caer London and at last London.

Lludd loved Llevelys best of all his brothers because he was a wise and discreet man. It came to pass that the king of France died without a male heir to rule. However, all his earthly possessions he left to his maiden daughter. Llevelys thought he could bring further glory and honor to the family by seeking the hand of the maiden. Together Llevelys and Lludd set forth to meet with the nobles of France. It was agreed that the maiden would marry Llevelys and that through her he would gain the crown of the kingdom. He ruled the land wisely and happily.

After a good amount of time, the island of Britain was struck with three plagues, the likes of which had never been known to the island. The first of the plagues was the arrival of the Coranians—a race of dwarves who could hear even a whisper that was caught by the wind. They could not be routed, because even the most discreet plans spoken in hushed tones became known to them by the very winds carrying voices.

The second plague was a great shriek heard throughout the land on every May Eve. So shrill was it that it cut through the hearts of all who heard it, causing men to lose their strength and women to lose their babies. It would leave the animals, land and waters barren.

The third plague was indeed perplexing. No matter how provision of food and drink were prepared and stored for the year of the king's court, after the feasting of the first night the storage areas would be bare the next day.

Greatly vexed by these plagues, Lludd sought the counsel of his vassal nobles. They advised him in ways that could be conveyed through sign and gesture so that their advice would not be heard by the Coranians. Seeking further counsel, Lludd journeyed across the waters to his brother Llevelys the king of France. The two met in the waters between Britain and France. Llevelys brought with him a long brass tube through which they could talk without fear of their words being carried by the wind to the Coranians.

Of the first plague, Llevelys told Lludd that he would give an insect that he should bruise in water, making an infusion. He was then to invite the Coranians to a feast where they would make peace. He was to cast the water over all the assembled, which would be as poison only to the Coranians.

Llevelys next addressed the second plague, which was the most egregious. He told Lludd that in his land there resides a red dragon that is one with the land and that there was a white dragon that was foreign to the land. He went on to say that the white dragon was striving to overcome the red dragon and the shriek that had been heard was the red dragon's fearful outcry. Llevelys told Lludd that he should measure the length and breadth, finding the exact center of the island. There he should place a cauldron with mead in the bottom. He should cover the cauldron with satin. There he would see the dragons fighting in the guise of great animals fighting. They would in time take the form of dragons in the air, finally transforming into pigs upon settling on the satin covering, sinking into the cauldron. They would drink the mead and fall into a deep slumber. He was to then tie them in the satin cloth and bury them in the Earth where they would not be disturbed. Indeed, if they remained buried the island would not succumb to any other plague.

Of the third plague, Llevelys said there was a mighty man of magic who would come at night to take all the food and drink. His stealth was due to an enchantment he laid on the folk. Llevelys told Lludd that he would catch the thief in the act and that he should challenge the mighty man.

Lludd returned to his land in a hasty manner. Immediately he invited the Coranians, dispatching them as had been discussed—sprinkling the prepared water on all who attended the feast. The Coranians immediately died while the Britons remained unharmed.

He then set a great banquet, setting himself to await the mighty man who would come to steal the bounty. As was anticipated by Llevelys, the thief showed himself at midnight. Lludd, being awake, engaged the man in battle. Lludd overcame the man who then begged for mercy. Lludd spared him as the man promised to atone by providing all that had been lost and more.

Lludd then set himself to the most egregious of the plagues and caused the island to be measured both length and width, finding the center to be in Oxford. There did he place the cauldron with mead and the satin covering. He sat through the night watching and just as had been said,

at long last came a great noise as two dragons—red and white—fought until they tired, falling upon the covering of the cauldron as two pigs. They drank deeply of the mead and fell into a slumber. Lludd folded the satin around them, bringing his stronghold Dinas Emrys in Yr Wyddfa (Snowden.) From that time, the great cry was not heard again.

Vortigern the disgraced

After a good amount of time Vortigern came to the throne of the Britons. It was during his time that the Scots and the Picts were making inroads into the kingdom. His efforts to thwart their raids and other harassments were to no avail. His forces could not match theirs. It was also at that time that three ships arrived from the north-lands. Two Saxon brothers, Horsa and Hengist, landed on the island. It was in them that Vortigern saw a solution to his problem. He would hire them as mercenaries to fight the Scots and the Picts. Vortigern approached Hengist, who assured him that his people were valiant men who indeed would vanquish the enemies of Vortigern.

A contract was made with the Saxon, whereupon Hengist sent for more men. He sent for his brother and his brother's sons—Octa and Ebusa—who arrived with forty ships filled with men. In short order they halted and drove back the Scots and the Picts. Before any realized it, the Saxons became a power in the island of the Britons, taking Kent as their own. The land began to slip from Vortigern's hands. These transgressions not being enough, Vortigern married Hengist's daughter and she bore him a son.

All of this being too much for the Britons, Vortigern gathered twelve wise men to advise him on how to resolve his predicament. Not seeing a good way out, they advised him to retire to the boundaries of the kingdom and there build a stronghold to defend himself, for surely the Saxon and his own people sought his demise.

The king heeded their advice, traveling through the kingdom and ending the journey at Dinas Emrys. It was here that Vortigern decided he would build a citadel from which he could defend himself. He dispatched his messenger to bring to him artificers, carpenters and stonemasons and he collected all the materials requisite to building. They began immediately to fabricate the fortress. All retired in the evening, then waking the following morning all the work done was gone,

all the supplies gone. They again began the project only to find that all was gone the next day. On the third try with the same result, Vortigern sent for his wisemen to consult on the problem. They advised that he must find a child born without a father. By putting him to death and sprinkling his blood on the foundations of the citadel, all would finally progress.

Vortigern immediately dispatched search parties to find the fatherless child that the wisemen spoke of. In short order the boy was found quite by accident. They heard two youth quarreling, the one calling the other a bastard fatherless child. Inquiring of the details with the boy's mother, she indeed confirmed that she had not lain with any man to conceive the boy.

The child was brought before Vortigern. The boy, in defiance, asked why he was brought before the king. The king recounted the recent events to the child and told him that he would be put to death and that his blood would be sprinkled on the foundations of the citadel. The child queried how the advice of this grim task was arrived at. The king explained that it was his wisemen who gave him advice. The boy asked if he might talk with the king's advisors.

The wisemen came before the king and the boy. The boy immediately asked them what was hidden beneath the ground. They were ashamed that they could not answer. The boy told them that buried beneath the foundation are two vases in a pool and that there was a tent and that in the tent were serpent dragons—one red and one white. They dug into the ground and found exactly as the boy had related. Having unearthed the tent with the dragons, the beasts began to fight each other. At length the red dragon, being weaker although recovering some strength, expelled the white one from the tent. The red dragon pursued the white one.

The boy then explained the mystery to the king and his wisemen. He told them that the pool represented the world and that the tent represented the kingdom. He told the king that the red serpent was of the island of the Britons and that the white was the dragon of the Saxons. He told them that the red dragon—the Britons—would vanquish the white dragon—the Saxons. He further advised the king to depart from Dinas Emrys, saying that he was not permitted to raise a citadel there and that he should seek another in other provinces.

After a short time, Vortigern engaged the Saxons. He did so four times but not for long—Vortigern died after the fourth battle. Before he died, he commanded that he be buried under the rock where the Saxons first landed. He said that although they might inhabit part of Britain, they would never remain. His people did not heed his wishes, neglecting to bury him where he commanded.

—GWION VRAN

Cassadaga—Central Florida's Spiritualist Community

Where Mayberry meets The Twilight Zone

THIS ENIGMATIC slogan appears on souvenir T-shirts and bumper stickers available in the Cassadaga gift shop. Cassadaga is a peaceful unincorporated area in rural Central Florida. The community is home to about 100 permanent residents. That's the Mayberry part. The tiny historic village is also the dwelling place for innumerable legends and spirits—that's the Twilight Zone part. Ghost walks, psychic readings, materializing mediums, séances with messages from the afterlife, spirit orbs and other various paranormal happenings are daily occurrences.

A walk along the narrow streets leaves an impression that nothing has changed since at least the 1930s. Most of the homes in Cassadaga were built in the late 19th to very early 20th centuries. The word Cassadaga derives from the Seneca language and means "rocks beneath the water." There is also a town called Cassadaga in upstate New York, adjacent to Lily Dale, another place which is a long-time mecca for Spiritualists and Spiritualism.

Spiritualism is a religion which was established on March 31, 1848 in Hydesville, New York. That's when three young sisters—Leah, Maggie and Katie Fox—began to communicate with the spirit world. This exciting event quickly drew worldwide attention and attracted millions of followers. Spiritualism is a religion, science and philosophy which offers comfort to those who grieve the dead and seek afterlife communication. Spiritualism's nine principles affirm that communication with the so-called dead is a fact and that existence and personal identity continues after the change called death.

Cassadaga, Florida was founded by George P. Colby (January 6, 1848– July 27, 1933), a spiritual healer and

114

clairvoyant medium from Pike, New York. It was 1875 when Colby's spirit guides—Seneca, the Philosopher and the Unknown—directed him to travel by train to Florida. He went by rail as far as Jacksonville then wandered inland until he found the location near a natural spring and beautiful lake, as described by the spirits. In 1880 he applied for a homestead grant which was awarded in 1894. He persuaded fellow Spiritualists from Lily Dale, New York to join him in establishing The Southern Cassadaga Camp Meeting Association on December 18, 1894. It began literally as a campground catering to those spending the winter in Florida before returning North for the summer!

The Association survives today as a the oldest continuously operating Spiritualist camp in the southeastern United States. Visitors can enjoy visiting C. Greene's Haunted Museum which houses an impressive collection of curiosities. Also of interest is The Cassadaga Hotel, which offers rooms and meals, The Cassadaga Bookstore, workshops and classes with a paranormal theme and personal sessions with resident mediums or spiritual healers. There are public services on Wednesday evenings and Sunday mornings in beautiful Colby Temple.

Here are the nine principles of Spiritualism. Usually these are read aloud during the services.

Declaration of Principles, from The National Association of Spiritualist Churches

1. We believe in Infinite Intelligence.
2. We believe that the phenomena of Nature, both physical and spiritual, are the expression of Infinite Intelligence.
3. We affirm that a correct understanding of such expression and living in accordance therewith, constitute true religion.
4. We affirm that the existence and personal identity of the individual continue after the change called death.
5. We affirm that communication with the so-called dead is a fact, scientifically proven by the phenomena of Spiritualism.
6. We believe that the highest morality is contained in the Golden Rule: "Do unto others as you would have them do unto you."
7. We affirm the moral responsibility of individuals, and that we make our own happiness or unhappiness as we obey or disobey Nature's physical and spiritual laws.
8. We affirm that the doorway to reformation is never closed against any soul here or hereafter.
9. We affirm that the precepts of Prophecy and Healing are Divine attributes proven through Mediumship.

—GRANIA LING

115

The Sunken Roads

Bostels, Holloways, Shuts and Grundels
Earth Journeys Over, Under and Round About

THE NEWEST of them are at least three hundred years old. Most date from the Iron Age, a period of prehistory which spanned 1100–600 BCE. They are the paths in modern Great Britain which grew into roadways, then eroded so far below the surface of the surrounding land that they have touched bedrock. Throughout many generations, countless wheels, hooves and feet have left creases reminiscent of the lines created in an aging face during the course of a lifetime—they have a unique and incomparable beauty. Intriguing traditions, customs and seasonal shifts over many centuries are recorded within these sunken roads. The most familiar word for them is probably *holloway*, which has evolved into a common Anglo-Saxon surname. Originally the word was *hola-weg* and can be translated in today's language to indicate a harrowed lane.

Many holloways began as routes for a pilgrimage, as ditches or ruts to mark a boundary or as the ways to marketplaces. Worn down over time, they became temporary riverbeds during rainy seasons when the rushing waters would expose more stones and tree roots—secrets erupting from beneath Earth's surface.

Holloways are most common in areas which have a soft stone surface like chalk, limestone or clay. In the UK the southernmost counties such as Essex, Dorset, Hampshire, Kent and East Anglia have the most holloways. They don't occur in the hard, rocky, mountainous areas like Scotland's Highlands.

The deepest holloways create an otherworldly journey for the hiker. These are mysterious shadowed ravines running far below the surface of the surrounding fields and forest lands. Their twisting routes are silent testimonies about the distant past. Sensitives who encounter them will sense presences, a mystical remembrance of other people who lived in another time. The spirit and essence of long forgotten individuals hover in the shadows and corners of the holloways. Witches who keep the old ways can especially appreciate exploring them.

—MARINA BRYONY

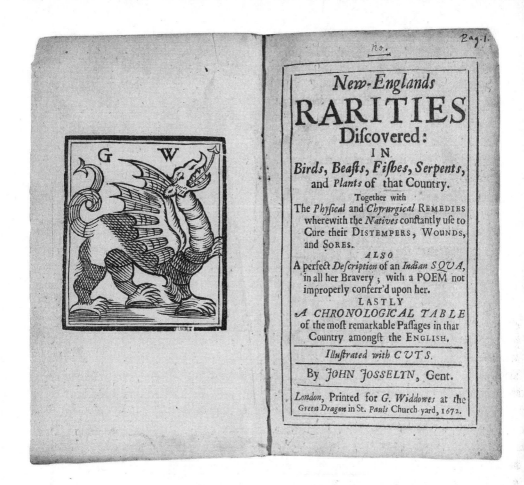

New-Englands
RARITIES
Difcovered:
I N.
Birds, Beaſts, Fiſhes, Serpents,
and *Plants* of that Country.
Together with
The *Phyſical* and *Chyrurgical* REMEDIES
wherewith the *Natives* conſtantly uſe to
Cure their DISTEMPERS, WOUNDS,
and SORES.
ALSO
A perfect *Deſcription* of an *Indian S QU A,*
in all her Bravery; with a POEM not
improperly conferr'd upon her.
LASTLY
A CHRONOLOGICAL TABLE
of the moſt remarkable Paſſages in that
Country amongſt the ENGLISH.

Illuſtrated with C U T S.

By *JOHN JOSSELYN*, Gent.

London, Printed for *G. Widdowes* at the
Green Dragon in St. *Pauls* Church-yard, 1672.

Native Remedies

from New-Englands Rarities Discovered: In Birds, Beasts,
Fishes, Serpents, and Plants of that Country. Together with the
Physical and Chyrurgical Remedies wherewith the Natives
constantly use to Cure their Distempers, Wounds, and Sores...
London, Printed for G. Widdowes, 1672.

WHEN THE ENGLISH colonists came to New England, they were as heavily loaded with cultural baggage as any other immigrant group. Religion is the most obvious example, but consider how tenacious immigrants can be even about replicating the cuisine of their homeland, whatever the challenge of unavailable ingredients or equipment. On the question of medicine, by and large the English remained loyal to the Hippocratic-Galenist tradition, importing the practices (i.e., humoral adjustment, phlebotomy,) drugs and herbs they were familiar with. There was even debate at the time as to whether European medicine was most appropriate for European bodies or if indigenous remedies were better in an alien context. There was general interest in discovering what New World fauna and flora might be of use, but from a European perspective. That Native medical knowledge could contribute much of value was discounted.

There was, however, one early observer who came to appreciate and benefit from the wisdom of the Native peoples, indigenous women in particular. This was the natural philosopher—the period term for scientist—and anti-Puritan John Josselyn, who wrote a book—*New-Englands Rarities Discovered*—in 1672 on what he learned from the Abenaki in Maine. As he states after his second voyage, "I resided eight years [1663–1671,] and made it my business to discover all along the Natural, Physical, and Chyrurgical Rarities of this New-found World."

Josselyn's natural survey is far more extensive than just on medicine, but was unique for the time in the credit given his local informants. It captures examples of indigenous physic before it was modified by the introduction of European plants and therapeutics.

One class of remedies that might be overlooked today but that was important for Native peoples were animal fats they used for salves, repellants and cosmetics. The preferred animal fat was bear grease, which, in addition to being a common

Hollow Leav'd Lavender.   Page 54.

cooking ingredient, was used to repel insects, preserve body heat and serve as hair pomade. Josselyn writes on page fourteen of *Rarities* that, "Their Grease is very good for Aches and Cold Swellings, the *Indians* anoint themselves therewith from top to toe, which hardens them against the cold weather." Of Wildcat—or "Ounce"— fat, Josselyn says on page sixteen, "Their Grease is soveraign for all manner of Aches and shrunk Sinews." "Sinew-shrunk" was when the sinew channel under the stomach was shrunk through excessive fatigue. Seal fat was used as a salve for scalds and sores and also burned as a fumigation to relieve hysteria, as Josselyn notes on page thirty-four.

Josselyn collected a great many botanical remedies. Examples from *Rarities* identified as part of the Native American *materia medica* include:

- "*Water Plantane*, here called *Water suck-leaves*" (*Alisma plantago-aquatica*) was used for burns and scalds, and "to draw Water out of swell'd Legs," à treatment for edema.
- "*White Hellibore* [*Veratrum viride*] …The *Indians* Cure their Wounds with it, anointing the Wound first with Raccoons greese, or Wild-Cats greese, and strewing upon it the powder of the Roots; and for Aches they scarifie the grieved part, and annoint it with one of the foresaid Oyls, then strew upon it the powder: The powder of the Root put into a hollow Tooth, is good for the Tooth-ach: The Root sliced thin and boyled in Vineager, is very good against *Herpes Milliaris*."
- "*For Scall'd-heads*. Of the Moss that grows at the roots of the white Oak the *Indesses* make a strong decoction, with which they help their *Papouses* or young Childrens scall'd Heads," (eczema of the scalp.)
- "*Board Pine* (white pine)… For *Stabbs*. The *Indians* make use of the Moss boiled in Spring Water, for Stabbs [wounds], pouring in the Liquor, and applying the boiled Moss well stamp'd or beaten betwixt two stones…*To take Fire out of*

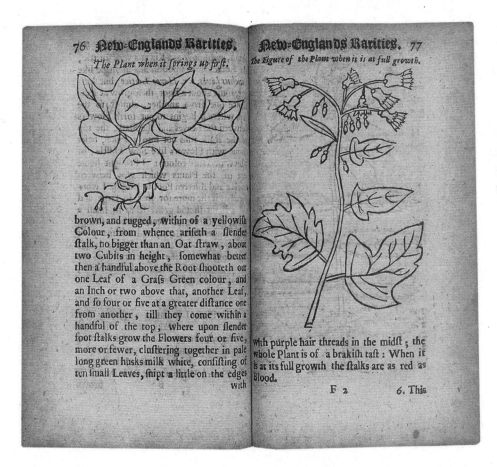

The Plant when it springs up first.

brown, and rugged, within of a yellowish Colour, from whence ariseth a slender stalk, no bigger than an Oat straw, about two Cubits in height, somewhat better then a handful above the Root shooteth out one Leaf of a Grass Green colour, and an Inch or two above that, another Leaf, and so four or five at a greater distance one from another, till they come within a handful of the top, where upon slender foot stalks grow the Flowers four or five, more or fewer, clustering together in pale long green husks milk white, consisting of ten small Leaves, snipt a little on the edges with

The Figure of the Plant when it is at full growth.

with purple hair threads in the midst; the whole Plant is of a brakish tast: When it is at its full growth the stalks are as red as Blood.

F 2   6. This

a Burn. One Christopher Luxe, a Fisher-man, having burnt his Knee Pan, was healed again by an Indian Webb, or Wife, (for so they call those Women that have Husbands;) She first made a strong decoction of Alder bark, with which she took out the Fire by Imbrocation, or letting of it drop upon the Sore, which would smoak notably with it; then she Playstered it with the Bark of *Board Pine*, or *Hemlock Tree*, boyled soft and stampt betwixt two stones, till it was as thin as brown Paper, and of the same Colour, she annointed the Playster with *Soyles* [seal's] *Oyl*, and the Sore likewise, then she laid it on warm, and sometimes she made use of the bark of the *Larch Tree*."

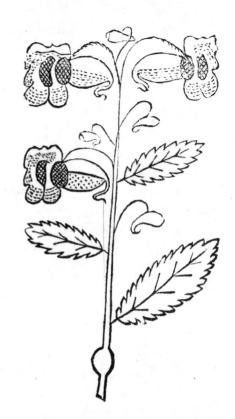

- "*For Stitches*. The Firr Tree, or Pitch Tree, the Tar that is made of all sorts of *Pitch Wood* is an excellent thing to take away those desperate Stitches of the Sides, which perpetually afflicteth those poor People that are stricken with the Plague of the Back."

- "*Cran Berry*, or *Bear Berry*...They are excellent against the Scurvy... "*For the heat in Feavers*. They are also good to allay the fervour of hot Diseases. The *Indians* and *English* use them much, boyling them with Sugar for Sauce to eat with their Meat; and it is a delicate Sauce, especially for roasted Mutton: Some make Tarts with them as with Goose Berries."

- "*To dissolve a Scirrhous Tumour*. An *Indian* dissolv'd a *Scirrhous Tumour* [A hard, fibrous, particularly invasive cancerous tumor] in the Arm and Hip, with a fomentation of Tobacco, applying afterwards the Herb stamp'd betwixt two stones."

- "*For Swellings of the Foot*. An *Indian* Webb, her Foot being very much swell'd and inflamed, asswaged the swelling, and took away the inflamation with our Garden or *English Patience* (*Rumex patientia*), the Roots roasted."

This last is an example of how the introduction of English plants would come to influence Native practice. By the nineteenth century, the two cultures' folk or popular remedies had undergone some integration, even as orthodox allopathic medicine left both behind.

—JIM BAKER

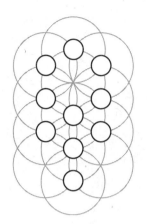

Twin Angels from Earth

"Enoch walked with Elohim and then he was gone because Elohim took him."

Genesis 5:24

THE ARCHANGELS Metatron and Sandalphon are twins—not by birth but in beginnings. Of all the hosts of heaven, these are the only two who were once human. Their function is to mediate the flow of energy and prayers between the realms. They are the two cherubim on the lid of the Ark of the Covenant, watching over the contract between mankind and the divine. They are Kether and Malkuth, the Crown and the Kingdom, and between them they oversee the currents of spiritual power as they transfer between the world of humans and the world of Gods.

Sandalphon

It is said that Sandalphon is the prophet Elijah, that after he arose to heaven in a chariot of fire, he was transformed into the angel. Wearing brown robes and holding a cornucopia

that represents the bounty of Earth, Sandalphon represents Malkuth, the lowest sephirah on the Tree of Life which corresponds to the physical world. He gathers the prayers of humans and delivers them to heaven, turning them into music to glorify the divine. The tallest of the angels, his head reaches paradise while his legs stretch so far down that his feet are rooted in the depths of Earth. In the magick circle, Sandalphon stands below the magician—between the magician and the earthly realm. Some magicians call on Sandalphon in the Lesser Banishing Ritual of the Pentagram in the same position.

Entreat Sandalphon for aid with material concerns, such as physical strength, health, financial stability, matters concerning the home and

for musical ability. You can honor Sandalphon by honoring Earth and protecting both land and water.

Metatron

The prophet Enoch was transformed into Metatron, the angel of the veil. The highest of the angels, he records all that happens on Earth and in heaven. He can be visualized wearing shimmering robes of blinding white, standing near a throne or sitting on one. In the key of Solomon he is, "the Great Angel Metatron, Who is the Prince of the Angels, and introduceth the souls before the face of God..." One of the proposed etymologies of his name translates to "near the throne." He is so close to God, in fact, that some have identified him as the "Ancient of Days" that came to Daniel, a figure more traditionally identified as YHVH. His name has the same gematria as *Shaddai*, further indicating that he stands with the divine.

As the archangel associated with Kether, the crown sephirah on the Tree of Life, Metatron directs the power and substance of the divine as it flows to Earth. In the magick circle, Metatron stands above the magician—between the magician and the realm of heaven—and can be called upon in the same space as an addition to the Lesser Banishing Ritual of the Pentagram as well.

You can honor Metatron by studying the *Book of Enoch* and engaging in spiritual practices. Call on Metatron and vibrate his name and energy to attain enlightenment and aid in spiritual endeavors.

—MAB BORDEN

Merry Meetings

A candle in the window, a fire on the hearth,
a discourse over tea…

MOTHER AND DAUGHTER Geraldine and Bali Beskin own the world's oldest independent esoteric bookshop. The Atlantis Bookshop in London was founded in 1922 and has had a considerable impact on modern Paganism and Witchcraft. The Witches' Almanac had the privilege of interviewing Geraldine Beskin as they mark their 100th anniversary in business.

What is it like having a 100-year-old business? Tell us about the bookshop.

The Atlantis Bookshop on Museum Street in London is in the heart of the city, next to the British Museum. This is where the streets are narrow and the architecture is quaint as most of it is between 150 and 300 years old. The street signs don't match, the police pass by on sunny days up on their fine horses as they exercise them. Tourists from all over the world drink in the two old pubs, eat fish and chips and visit us in the most magical shop in London. We suit our surroundings as we, too, are little and cute. But as they see our besoms—our broomsticks—outside, they begin to realise we are different. During 2022 the huge gold balloons showing 100 began to tell our story as we were celebrating our centenary as sellers of magic, Witchcraft, and everything from alchemy to Zoroastrianism, to generations of people.

Does an old bookshop selling magical items feel incongruous in modern London?

Bali and I are very proud of our past but don't live in it. We are surrounded by wonderfully designed books in jolly colours with amazing covers. The virtually universal acceptance of the existence of magic, the power of spells, and the benefits of mediation and good living have made publishers sit up and take notice of the power of the Pagan purchasers. TikTok and other social media have demonstrated to us all what to do and how to do it. I must admit sometimes I think they cannot be serious—but they are.

Atlantis Bookshop was founded in 1922. Does it have any ties to the occult revival going on at that time?

Our building was built in 1888, the very year The Hermetic Order of the Golden Dawn began—just about a mile away! Those esoteric pioneers would have

seen the shop being built and we like to think they would have pushed the door open using the handles we use today! As we are 50 yards from the British Museum which housed the British Library where they all studied magical manuscripts, and there seems to have always been a café next door, it is quite likely they trod our floorboards. We have the original oil painting of Samuel MacGregor Mathers—one of the three founders of the Golden Dawn hanging in the shop with some original working tools from the Order.

How did magic become your family business?

Our family is unique as we are known to be third and fourth generations of Witches. My father was from a different line to my mother and having 'blood' from two hereditary lines is most unusual. We have seen fashions change in the Craft of course and not least the status of 'Hereditaries' like Bali and I, as at one stage if you weren't Gardnerian or Alexandrian you were dismissed. The family has never been bothered by that as we just stay true to what we know and get on with it. My practice is different from my mother's and Bali's is different in turn. Not in ways that matter but in the little touches. One of us can sprinkle fairy dust on a cheese sandwich and make it seem like a feast while the other of us—me—is likely to have run out of matches. I have often told the tale of opening my box of kit and seeing with fresh eyes how I had let my standards slip. When was the last time I had ironed that cloth? Polished those candlesticks? Put the incense in order? When I'm tidy, I'm

by the mystical notes of the TS and travelled the world seeking gurus and holy men. He was Paul Brunton and he more or less settled in the USA and people sat at his itchy feet for many years and read his many books. The other chap was Michael Houghton, also known as Michael Juste when he published his poetry. He stayed behind and carried on with Atlantis and knew absolutely everybody. Manly P Hall visited during his world tour. Israel Regardie revisited us in the 1980s and spent time in our basement complaining of the cold. Bali insists she had lunch with him as I was pregnant with her at the time! The visionary artist Austin Osman Spare was a friend of Michael Houghton's and I found the first two images in my collection by him in the store room in the 1970s. I curated my first exhibition of his work in 1987 and Bali and I have had four more shows of his work so far. Watch this space!*

very tidy. I then clean and prepare things I will need on a need-to-use basis for a whole year as a reminder not to be so lazy! As Doreen Valiente said to me, "Only your best is good enough, Geraldine." She was a darling and my mother and she would talk the afternoon away many atime.*

So many people have connections to it or have heard of it—it's almost like a pilgrimage. Can you explain for our readers why The Atlantis Bookshop has an important place in modern magical history?

The Atlantis Bookshop's history is unique and important in the last 100 years of the Western Mysteries. It was begun by two earnest young men who joined the Theosophical Society, as everyone did back in the day. It was the place to meet and discuss everything with men and women. One of our young men became captivated

Tell us about the space itself. What is it like? Does it feel like it holds onto the magic of the past?

We are a small shop with a smaller room in the basement but that little space holds enormous religious significance. It is where Michael Houghton allowed Gerald Gardner and his coven to meet. There had been an enormous scandal during World War 2 when a very good Spiritualist Medium named Helen Duncan was so accurate she was presumed to be a danger to state security and she was tried as a Witch in the highest court in the land. That put the word back into people's minds and Gardner had to meet clandestinely here on Museum Street as Witchcraft was illegal in England until 1951.

Witchcraft is the only religion the United Kingdom has given to the world and Bali and I are so very proud of the role Michael and the other brave pioneers played in continuing it at potentially great personal cost. The Gardner Room is used for workshops, art exhibitions and is open every day for people to enjoy. We have a little Cabinet of Curiosities in there and during the Centennial year we displayed a crystal ball owned by someone who took part in the legendary ritual to repel Hitler in 1939. Gardner and his friends were too old to be in the Forces but active service can take many forms.

What other magical giants of history have had connections with The Atlantis Bookshop?

Mention has to be made of Aleister Crowley as he was another of Michael's friends. He was very honest about his life as a sexual being, a poet, the best magician of the 20th century, appalling and funny, climber of K2—the rival to Everest as the highest mountain in the world—and so much more besides. Our little publishing house, Neptune Press, produced an edition of his 777 in the 1950s and we did some reprints in the 1970s with 'groovy' typefaces. He inherited a small fortune when he was 21 and spent it travelling the world, studying magic and mysticism with the peoples of many lands, as they actually knew what they were talking about. He came down to Earth with a bump when the cash ran out so became a prolific author to try and keep the idea of Crowleyanity—loosely the Law of Thelema, the Law of Do what Thou Wilt—alive. Seventy-five years after his death, love him or hate him, everyone has an opinion of him so it kind of worked! He would have been so embarrassing to go to the pub with but so deeply fascinating, too.

A painting of Mathers, a room used as a covenstead by Gardner—those are significant representations of the connection between the magic practiced today and its modern forebears. Are there any others?

Another item we have is the crystal ball owned by Dion Fortune. She wrote Mystical Qabala *which is the clearest book on the subject you could ever read, several books on magic and quite a few novels. What makes her important still is that she taught people, so by the time she came to write her books, she knew the questions people wanted to have answered. Dion Fortune and members of her Society of Inner Light are also key as some of the people who put our beloved Glastonbury back on the map. It was they who tried so hard to reawaken the spirit of Albion, the land of King Arthur, the home of the Grail, and told everyone that Glastonbury, the Isle of Avalon, is the mystical heart of Britain.*

Is there a particular kind of magical customer you cater to?

We treat all our customers as equals so have never elevated one group above another. In the eyes of the Gods we are all one and if our hearts are pure we are given their attention and protection. We love people who are just setting out on their esoteric journey as they ask the hardest questions! None of us know it all and never, ever be scared to ask, whether you are attending a Zoom meeting or a 'live' gathering—or buying a book from a shop. We don't know what we know until we need to give an answer so it keeps us on our toes! I have lectured variously in the States, Canada, Australia and Europe and sometimes a shy person has asked something that has us all scratching our heads. No one starts anything because they know all about it so keep reading and you will be more confident and be pleased that you can help someone else.

Thank you so much for chatting with us! What last words do you have for our readers?

Bali and I wish you all very well. We hope you are of good cheer and take great pleasure in the miracle of Life in all its forms from the grass growing through the paving stones to us, the cleverest and necessarily most responsible organisms on our lovely Gaia. She knows best and every tiny green footprint we leave on her remarkable body is welcomed by her. Be kind to yourself and to others, walk towards the Light and know you are not alone but in very good company.

PAMELA COLMAN SMITH

First Lady of the Tarot

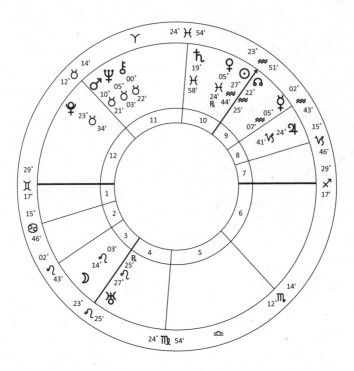

Pamela Colman Smith was born near London, England on February 16, 1878. The astrological indicators of her birth foreshadowed her unusual life. Unexpected circumstances and eccentric or original personal choices often are linked to the lives of those born with the Sun in Aquarius. She came into the world just hours before a North Node eclipse of the Full Moon in Leo. Often a person whose life has a lasting impact will be born near an eclipse. Her legacy is the 78 paintings of the Tarot cards in the Rider-Waite Tarot deck. Her illustrations have touched the emotions and stimulated the intuitive perceptions of millions of people for over a century. Pamela Colman Smith was the first metaphysical practitioner to illustrate the 56 minor arcana cards in addition to the 22 major arcana cards.

Pamela had a spritely, lively personality which earned her the nickname "Pixie." Photographs certainly support the whispered rumors that she was biracial. Some say that her mother was Jamaican and her father was British. Other accounts describe her as being born of American parents. Her exotic appearance and eclectic dress even led to speculation that she must be Asian, perhaps Chinese. She grew up between England, Jamaica and New York. As is true with many Aquarians, Pixie had a wide circle of friends which included William Butler Yeats, his son Jack Yeats, Alfred Steiglitz, Ellen Terry and other theatrical and literary personalities of the late 19th and early 20th centuries. Pamela was an initiate of the Hermetic Order of the Golden Dawn, and worked closely with noted occultist A.E. Waite.

Pamela's Mercury was in Aquarius revealing her brilliance and originality, along with her Aquarian Sun and North Node. Her Sun was in mutual reception with retrograde Uranus in Leo, giving her the unusual natal marker of a retrograde Sun. (Note: Mutual receptions occur when planets are in each other's ruling signs. They are considered very fortunate and enriching as a rule, bringing a multi-dimensional quality and even shapeshifting capabilities. Pamela Colman Smith's horoscope actually has two mutual receptions, both involving retrograde planets.) The retrograde Sun-Uranus mutual reception points to many unexpected twists and turns during the course of her life.

She was an artist, a theatrical designer and gifted storyteller. Her formal art training at the famous Pratt Institute in New York helped Pixie to develop her natural talents. The years she spent in Jamaica allowed her to learn traditional folk tales which she told while performing in West Indies-style costumes upon returning to England. Her Leo Moon was conjunct Uranus. This powerful Leo influence reveals her charisma, theatrical flair and dramatic ability. She made miniature theaters with characters she cut from cardboard and painted with tempera to include with her storytelling sessions. Her performances were in high demand for several seasons in turn of the 20th century London. Pamela also wrote and illustrated a number of books

and pamphlets. She was born with Venus retrograde in Pisces, in mutual reception with Neptune in Taurus. Her Mars is conjunct Neptune in Taurus, an aspect which has been especially linked with mystical talent and creative visualization. Sometimes a Mars-Neptune conjunction is called "the Lamp of Aladdin" aspect or the sign of a "White Witch." The Pisces influence also enhances her creativity and insight into the paranormal.

Her Chiron and Pluto complete a four-planet stellium in Taurus with Neptune and Mars. This Taurus pattern accents the significance of music in her life. She would paint visionary impressions which came to her while listening to Chopin, Bach, Beethoven and Debussy. By 1903 her work earned critical acclaim and she sold thirty-three paintings at a single gallery exhibition in New York. In 1909 Arthur Edward Waite guided her in undertaking the illustration of what was to become the most famous Tarot deck of all time. Her fanciful imagination, affinity for ritual and the occult are evident in this impressive work. Pamela's name does not appear on the deck though. William Rider, the deck's publisher and Waite, who authored a text book of Tarot interpretation, received the acclaim and most of the money for this project. Pamela received only a token payment, which left her feeling discouraged and disillusioned. Although both sides of her family were quite affluent and prominent, she struggled with financial insecurity for most of her life. This was apparently sparked by her own poor monetary choices.

As is often the case with a retrograde Venus, she never married. She shared housing with a female roommate name Nora Lake for many years. Pamela's Taurus planets square both the Leo and Aquarius placements. This creates a difficult fixed T-square in her birth chart. Those fixed sign aspects along with her natal Saturn in impractical Pisces reveal the extreme financial hardship which she endured and her poor business decisions. After World War I she received a substantial inheritance from an uncle. She used it to take a long-term lease on a large property at the seaside to start an artists' colony called The Lizard. This proved to be a most unproductive venture. Pamela became a devout Catholic. Her natal Jupiter in Capricorn reflects this devotion to traditional faith and religious practices. She established a church on the leased property which she called "Our Lady of the Lizard" and began to make a meager living by offering vacation accommodations to Catholic priests.

By the time World War II began her physical health and her financial situation were in extreme decline. She was forced to leave the leased property. She and her companion moved first to Exeter where they lived with Nora Lake's family. Later they moved to Bude, Cornwall. Pamela continued to produce stories and artwork, but had little commercial success. Surviving correspondence from this time period reflects her futile attempts to collect financial remuneration. Her letters are filled with her requests for money. Her debts mounted. She became bedridden. When she died on September 18, 1951 at age 73, Pamela Colman Smith was penniless and nearly forgotten. Her possessions were auctioned off to satisfy her debts. Much of her work has disappeared. There was nothing at all remaining to leave an inheritance for her longtime companion, as she wished. There was no obituary published, no memorial service or grave marker to honor her life, a life which held such early promise.

It is a delight and surprise to those who follow her story today to see that Pamela Colman Smith's Tarot deck has endured. Her visionary talent has also resurfaced in the rediscovery of some of her art and literature. She continues to inspire succeeding generations of those who would follow a magical life.

—DIKKI-JO MULLEN

131

Pamela Colman Smith
Born Corrine Mary Pamela Colman Smith
Saturday, February 16, 1878
London, England
(born in Pimlico or Heston, Middlesex,
now parts of the greater London metro area)
12:00 noon GMT chart used—birth time unavailable

Data Table
Tropical Placidus Houses

Sun 27 Aquarius 44—10th house
Mutual Reception with Uranus in Leo

Moon 14 Leo 03—3rd house

Mercury 05 Aquarius 07—9th house

Venus 05 Pisces 24—10th house (retrograde)
Mutual Reception with Neptune in Taurus

Mars 10 Taurus 21—11th house

Jupiter 24 Capricorn 41—8th house

Saturn 19 Pisces 58—10th house

Uranus 27 Leo 25—4th house (retrograde)

Neptune 5 Taurus 03—11th house

Pluto 23 Taurus 34—12th house

Chiron 00 Taurus 22—11th house

North Moon Node 22 Aquarius 25—9th house

Ascendant (rising sign) is 29 Gemini 17

Death in the Cemetery

CEMETERIES ARE full of death, but at what point does a soul actually die?

While human souls may live on again and again in other physical bodies, consider the time spent in just one human life; the physical body, the physical death: the lingering memory of those who knew the living person, the physical grave or records of the previously living person and finally the complete loss of knowledge that the person ever lived.

To illustrate this, take a walk into a modern, "living" cemetery, and you will meet the people who have recently been buried. The grave may have fresh or still disturbed soil which has not yet grown new grass, indicating that a new resident has arrived. There may not even be a marking stone or monument present yet, as the living have not had the chance to manufacture the permanent memorial for the dead. Continue walking and you may come across graves that have been marked and grown over but now proudly show small tokens from their still living loved ones, such as flowers, small sentimental articles like stuffed animals, religious items, photographs—all talismans designed to keep a loving connection between the living and the dead. These souls are kept alive by the direct energy of the living ones who knew them well.

As you continue your walk, you begin to stray into an older section of

the cemetery. The souls located just beneath your feet have no direct living acquaintances anymore. However, their names—and in some instances titles—remind the living of who they are. Some names may be well known for either local or national events due to their living contributions—positively or negatively—during their tenure on Earth. Some will be recognized based on their title, fraternity, symbolism or service. These graves and names tend to live on if they were veterans, political or religious leaders, community founders and the like. You may celebrate formal remembrances of these people annually, such as reading the names of veterans on Memorial Day, or naming a street, school or major building after them. In this way they continue to live on by the memories of many, but seldom any who actually knew them beyond the contribution that has sealed their name with an event. Many names will just be a curiosity with little known about who they were or what life they experienced. Some of these names may seem quaint, antiquated and other-timely, increasing the disconnect from the dead with the living. Quite a few will simply be identified as "Son," "Daughter," or, sadly, only as "Child." Even this shows a disconnect with the past lives, as most will remark that this was a common occurrence way back then.

Graves can be filled with symbolism for those who know what to look for, which is another means to identify the dead with their deep beliefs or personalities. Religious symbolism is

the most common, however fraternal symbols such as the compass and square of Freemasonry, three chain links of the Odd Fellows and fez and sword of the Shriners are also common. Of occult symbolism—such as an ouroboros (a snake eating its tail,) winged hourglass (time running out,) torches both upright and downturned, broken columns and pineapples— entire books have been written about what these represent. "Sadly society seems to have forgotten what was once understood by many.

Many of the dead will have no markers at all, but their memories may live on in obscure written records hidden deep in the vaults of the libraries of the world, or other similar archived tombs. Sometimes a single large cenotaph will be placed instead of a grave to mark the physical memory of where someone once lived but is not buried. Ships lost at sea with all hands, missing soldiers and persons or the general memory of masses of people lost during wars, genocides or crusades may fall under this description.

The opposite of a cenotaph may be seen in the large catacombs or cathedrals found in many older cities around the world. Here the bones of thousands if not millions of the dead are clearly seen and artistically arranged to be part of the structure itself. Little or nothing is known about the souls for whom these bones once provided support for their thriving bodies, but in some way an unfamiliar memory still clings to life.

A further example of finding the remains of the unknown is seen in the mummified bodies of Egyptian, Asian and South American cultures. Some of these—such as Tutankhamun—are well known. Most are completely forgotten to memory. The "remains" left behind from the eruption of Mt. Vesuvius are hollows in the solidified ash formed by those who perished, which were found and then filled in with plaster to form casts of the victims. Still in the positions in which they succumbed, they are an extreme example of past lives still remaining in the world of the living.

For most of humanity, however, there is absolutely nothing remaining in the physical sense to leave a memory of the lives of those who once experienced this Earth. These souls are the truly dead and are only the small brushes of a breeze on a Spring day, a single drop of rain, or the dust riding a sunbeam in the morning. Or perhaps they have been freed and are alive and well now, occupying a living body close to you.

—JOHN M. NUTTALL

The Six Swans

ONCE UPON A TIME, a certain king was hunting in a great forest, and he chased a wild beast so eagerly that none of his attendants could follow him. When evening drew near he stopped and looked around him, and then he saw that he had lost his way. He sought a way out, but could find none. Then he perceived an aged woman with a head which nodded perpetually, who came towards him, but she was a witch. Good woman, said he to her, can you not show me the way through the forest. Oh, yes, lord king, she answered, that I certainly can, but on one condition, and if you do not fulfil that, you will never get out of the forest, and will die of hunger in it.

What kind of condition is it, asked the king. I have a daughter, said the old woman, who is as beautiful as anyone in the world, and well deserves to be your consort, and if you will make her your queen, I will show you the way out of the forest. In the anguish of his heart the king consented, and the old woman led him to her little hut, where her daughter was sitting by the fire. She received the king as if she had been expecting him, and he saw that she was very beautiful, but still she did not please him, and he could not look at her without secret horror. After he had taken the maiden up on his horse, the old woman showed him the way, and the king reached his royal palace again, where the wedding was celebrated.

The king had already been married once, and had by his first wife, seven children, six boys and a girl, whom he loved better than anything else in the world. As he now feared that the stepmother might not treat them well, and even do them some injury, he took

little shirts and went into the forest, and the ball showed her the way.

The children, who saw from a distance that someone was approaching, thought that their dear father was coming to them, and full of joy, ran to meet him. Then she threw one of the little shirts over each of them, and no sooner had the shirts touched their bodies than they were changed into swans, and flew away over the forest. The queen went home quite delighted, and thought she had got rid of her step-children, but the girl had not run out with her brothers, and the queen knew nothing about her.

Next day the king went to visit his children, but he found no one but the little girl. Where are your brothers, asked the king. Alas, dear father, she answered, they have gone away and left me alone, and she told him that she had seen from her little window how her brothers had flown away over the forest in the shape of swans, and she showed him the feathers, which they had let fall in the courtyard, and which she had picked up.

The king mourned, but he did not think that the queen had done this wicked deed, and as he feared that the girl would also be stolen away from him, he wanted to take her away with him. But she was afraid of her step-mother, and entreated the king to let her stay just this one night more in the forest castle.

them to a lonely castle which stood in the midst of a forest. It lay so concealed, and the way was so difficult to find that he himself would not have found it, if a wise woman had not given him a ball of yarn with wonderful properties. When he threw it down before him, it unrolled itself and showed him his path.

The king, however, went so frequently away to his dear children that the queen observed his absence, she was curious and wanted to know what he did when he was quite alone in the forest. She gave a great deal of money to his servants, and they betrayed the secret to her, and told her likewise of the ball which alone could point out the way. And now she knew no rest until she had learnt where the king kept the ball of yarn, and then she made little shirts of white silk, and as she had learnt the art of witchcraft from her mother, she sewed a charm inside them. And once when the king had ridden forth to hunt, she took the

The poor girl thought, I can no longer stay here. I will go and seek my brothers. And when night came, she ran away, and went straight into the forest. She walked the whole night long, and next day also without stopping, until she could go no farther for weariness. Then she saw a forest-hut, and went into it, and found a room with six little beds, but she did not venture to get into one of them, but crept under one, and lay down on the hard ground, intending to pass the night there. Just before sunset, however, she heard a rustling, and saw six swans come flying in at the window. They alighted on the ground and blew at each other, and blew all the feathers off, and their swans' skins stripped off like a shirt. Then the maiden looked at them and recognized her brothers, was glad and crept forth from beneath the bed. The brothers were not less delighted to see their little sister, but their joy was of short duration. Here you cannot abide, they said to her. This is a shelter for robbers, if they come home and find you, they will kill you. But can you not protect me, asked the little sister. No, they replied, only for one quarter of an hour each evening can we lay aside our swans' skins and have during that time our human form, after that, we are once more turned into swans.

The little sister wept and said, can you not be set free. Alas, no, they answered, the conditions are too hard. For six years you may neither speak nor laugh, and in that time you must sew together six little shirts of starwort for us. And if one single word falls from your lips, all your work will be lost. And when the brothers had said this, the quarter of an hour was over, and they flew out of the window again as swans.

The maiden, however, firmly resolved to deliver her brothers, even if it should cost her her life. She left the hut, went into the midst of the forest, seated herself on a tree, and there passed the night. Next morning she went out and gathered starwort and began to sew. She

could not speak to anyone, and she had no inclination to laugh, she sat there and looked at nothing but her work.

When she had already spent a long time there it came to pass that the king of the country was hunting in the forest, and his huntsmen came to the tree on which the maiden was sitting. They called to her and said, who are you. But she made no answer. Come down to us, said they. We will not do you any harm. She only shook her head. As they pressed her further with questions she threw her golden necklace down to them, and thought to content them thus. They, however, did not cease, and then she threw her girdle down to them, and as this also was to no purpose, her garters, and by degrees everything that she had on that she could do without until she had nothing left but her shift.

The huntsmen, however, did not let themselves be turned aside by that, but climbed the tree and fetched the maiden down and led her before the king. The king asked, who are you. What are you doing on the tree. But she did not answer. He put the question in every language that he

knew, but she remained as mute as a fish. As she was so beautiful, the king's heart was touched, and he was smitten with a great love for her. He put his mantle on her, took her before him on his horse, and carried her to his castle. Then he caused her to be dressed in rich garments, and she shone in her beauty like bright daylight, but no word could be drawn from her. He placed her by his side at table, and her modest bearing and courtesy pleased him so much that he said, she is the one whom I wish to marry, and no other woman in the world. And after some days he united himself to her.

The king, however, had a wicked mother who was dissatisfied with this marriage and spoke ill of the young queen. Who knows, said she, from whence the creature who can't speak, comes. She is not worthy of a king. After a year had passed, when the queen brought her first child into the world, the old woman took it away from her, and smeared her mouth with blood as she slept. Then she went to the king and accused the queen of being a man-eater. The king would not believe it, and would not suffer anyone to do her any injury. She, however, sat continually sewing at the shirts, and cared for nothing else.

The next time, when she again bore a beautiful boy, the false mother-in-law used the same treachery, but the king could not bring himself to give credit to her words. He said, she is too pious and good to do anything of that kind, if she were not dumb, and could defend herself, her innocence would come to light.

But when the old woman stole away the newly-born child for the third time, and accused the queen, who did not utter one word of defence, the king could do no otherwise than deliver her over to justice, and she was sentenced to suffer death by fire.

When the day came for the sentence to be carried out, it was the last day of the six years during which she was not to speak or laugh, and she had delivered her dear brothers from the power of the enchantment. The six shirts were ready, only the left sleeve of the sixth was wanting. When, therefore, she was led to the stake, she laid the shirts on her arm, and when she stood on high and the fire was just going to be lighted, she looked around and six swans came flying through the air towards her. Then she saw that her deliverance was near, and her heart leapt with joy. The swans swept towards her and sank down so that they were touched by them, their swans' skins fell off, and her brothers stood in their own bodily form before her, and were vigorous and handsome. The youngest only lacked his left arm, and had in the place of it a swan's wing on his shoulder. They embraced and kissed each other, and the queen went to the king, who was greatly moved, and she began to speak and said, dearest husband, now I may speak and declare to you that I am innocent, and falsely accused. And she told him of the treachery of the old woman who had taken away her three children and hidden them.

Then to the great joy of the king they were brought thither, and as a punishment, the wicked mother-in-law was bound to the stake, and burnt to ashes. But the king and the queen with her six brothers lived many years in happiness and peace.

Kites, Lines and Gates

Silent and Mysterious Messages in the Desert

GEOGLYPHS—they are best viewed from above. Aerial photographs taken either from space by satellites or by cameras attached to airplanes and hot air balloons reveal structures dotting desert areas on the Earth's surface. They are, to say the least, massive and ancient. Aerial archeologists compare them in size to football fields. Although just observed recently, scientists estimate many to have been around for 9,000 years or even longer.

They can be found in deserts in various parts of the world, from the desert plains of the Rio Grande de Nasca river basin in South America to the vast and unwelcoming volcanic field of Harrat Khabar in the Arabian Peninsula, to the deserts in Kazakhstan and Uzbekistan. Some have been uncovered because climate change is impacting the shifting

of sands. Others are in areas so remote that even in the 21st Century technology and travel are just now allowing them to be noticed. Collectively they are called geoglyphs, structures built into the Earth. Built by prehistoric people, the manmade constructions are sometimes incorporated into areas formed by natural events such as earthquakes or volcanic eruptions. These mysterious structures are intriguing. Who built them and why? What messages might they have?

The folklore of indigenous peoples—especially that of the nomadic desert Bedouins—has spoken of them for untold generations. However, they have just become widely noticed since World War I and the advent of airplanes. The structures have been called "The Works of Old Men" in the oldest legends. With the advent of more sophisticated methods of observation at least 80 to 100 more have been discovered since the turn of the 21st Century. Archeologists anticipate finding many new ones.

It was the Royal Airforce that first dubbed them "kites" because that is what they resemble from the sky. The gates are flat areas suggesting doorways. These are found on top of the kites in some instances—in others cases the gates are separate. The earthworks are the lasting testimonies of societies which existed in the mists of time. They are reminders which stretch across history. In probing them, primitive tools, human and animal remains and other hints of long ago human presences have been found.

Some appear to have been sites dedicated to rituals. Others might have been elaborate tombs or corrals used to contain the first domesticated cattle and other animals. Some appear to have been slaughter pits into which herds of wild animals, such as gazelles, were driven to be killed. Many of the kites are located along routes once used during animal migrations. The greatest concentration of geoglyphs is found in areas which were once wet with dense, fertile vegetation. Prior to long ago climate changes, these now-barren deserts supported the earliest civilizations which thrived in parts of what is now Syria and Jordan.

The famous Nazca Lines are a collection of vast geoglyphs created from stones and colored sand located in the Nazca Desert in southern Peru. With the availability of drones, these figures which feature animals and other objects can be observed. There has been some speculation that the Nazca Lines marked landing places for aliens, as references for space travelers. These forms appear to have been created much more recently than the geoglyphs in the middle East. Archeologists have dated them to about 500 BCE to 500 CE.

South American mystics and astrologers have developed a system of astrological birth signs connected to the Nazca Lines. Consult the Spirituality section in this year's Presage forecast for your own birth sign for an interpretation of what the Nazca Zodiac means to you. Here are the twelve geoglyphs included in the Nazca Zodiac. Meditating on the symbols connected with the zodiac signs might bring insights into what the messages of these earthworks could offer today's seekers. When all the data is examined, no one really knows exactly what the geoglyphs mean, only that they have been here for a very long time and were created with much care and effort. They obviously hold great significance.

The Nazca Zodiac
Aries—The Dog
Taurus—The Hand
Gemini—The Tree
Cancer—The Lizard
Leo—The Iguana
Virgo—The Spider
Libra—The Condor
Scorpio—The Monkey
Sagittarius—The Hummingbird
Capricorn—The Frigate Bird
Aquarius—The Root
Pisces—The Fish

—DIKKI-JO MULLEN

View of the Celestial Influx on the Body of Man, as illustrated in Culpeper's Family Physician, and Sibley's Occult Sciences.

IT IS SIMPLE, in theory at least, to find the usefulness of any herb once its astrological significance has been ascertained. In addition to knowing which parts of the body come under the dominion of each zodiacal sign, it is necessary to also know the planet whose special patronage each herb enjoys. This information can be gleaned from most older herbals, but for ease of reference the following table shows some common herbs and their ruling planets. Further details concerning the medicinal use of these and other herbs may be found in the herbal Materia Medica that forms Chapter 9 of *The Magic of Herbs*.

SUN

Burnet, celandine, centaury, chamomile, chicory, eyebright, heartsease, marigold, mistletoe, pimpernel, rosemary, saffron, St. John's Wort, sundew, viper's bugloss.

MOON

Adder's tongue, chickweed, cleavers (goosegrass), loosestrife, privet, purslane, rose (white), watercress, white poppy, willow.

MERCURY

Dill, fennel, hazel, honeysuckle, lily-of-the-valley, maidenhair, marjoram, mulberry, parsley, southernwood, vervain.

VENUS

Alder, birch, blackberry, burdock, coltsfoot, cowslip, daisy, elder, fennel, foxglove, ground ivy, groundsel, marshmallow, meadowsweet, mint, mugwort, periwinkle, plantain, primrose, sanicle, sea holly, sorrel, tansy, thyme, valerian, vervain, violet, yarrow.

MARS

Basil, broom, hawthorn, lesser celandine, stonecrop, thistle, toadflax, wormwood.

JUPITER

Agrimony, balm, betony, borage, chervil, chestnut, cinquefoil, dandelion, dock, houseleek, hyssop, rose (red), sage, thistle.

SATURN

Bistort, comfrey, hemlock, henbane, ivy, knapweed, moss, mullein, nightshade.

But how does this list of herbs and their planetary rulers inform magic and medicine? Take, for example, the lunar herbs. As Cancer is ruled by the Moon, some lunar herbs cure affliction in bodily parts ruled by Cancer. Others, however, being sacred to the Moon in her role as Mistress of the Night, are soporifics and can be used to aid in sleep.

It should be mentioned too that dedicated followers of the system will check on planetary conditions even before they set about harvesting their plants. By so doing they hope to ensure that the planet linked with the herb being gathered is not ill placed in relation to its neighbours on the day in question. The theory is that if the planet were adversely positioned, the power of the herb would be sympathetically depleted. However, collecting herbs is enough trouble without bothering at the same time about the precise arrangement of the heavens.

—DAVID CONWAY

Excerpted from *Magic of Herbs* which is available at TheWitchesAlmanac.com/products/the-magic-of-herbs/

Superstition Mountain and the Legend of the Lost Dutchman

THERE ARE extreme dust storms which sometimes plague and sicken the residents of Phoenix, Arizona. The dust clouds originate over sixty miles away, carried, it is said, by the sinister winds from the Superstition Mountains. The winds blow from deep within the Earth through a subterranean hole. Apache elders and story tellers speak of this hole.

The opening is believed to lead directly into the lower world, to Hell.

The Superstition Mountains are a mountain range located in Eastern Arizona along one side of an expansive desert plain. The mountain range is anchored by one large peak which is called Superstition Mountain. Traveling toward this mountain across the desert

from the metropolitan area of Phoenix, there is a sense that some supernatural presence is definitely stirring. The area is quiet and sparsely populated. The desert climate is stark. Apache Junction, the nearest town, offers a museum with artifacts and information about visiting the federally designated Superstition Wilderness area, including the enigmatic history of The Lost Dutchman's Gold Mine.

Hikers can explore many walking trails of different lengths. The most popular ones are the Peralta trail head and The Lost Dutchman State Park. The Peralta is named for a prominent Mexican mining family who became very wealthy upon discovering gold in the area. The Lost Dutchman refers to a legendary treasure of over two million dollars' worth of gold rumored to be hidden in the mountains.

The allure of treasure hunting, of retrieving and claiming the mother lode has captured the hearts and minds of many ever since October 25th of 1891. That was when one Jacob Waltz—a German immigrant and prospector—died of pneumonia in his boarding house. Jacob Waltz was born on September 2, 1810 near Stuttgart, Germany. His family was quite well to do and Jacob was very well educated with a university degree. He became ill following being treed by a flood. His landlady Julia Thomas cared for him. On his deathbed Jacob gave her a hand-drawn map and a series of clues which he said would lead her to the treasure. The clues are cryptic but do hint at landmarks which might be significant. One clue reads, "from the ridge above my mine, you can see

the Military Trail, but from the Trail, you cannot see my mine. Follow the North running canyon to the Salt River." Weaver's Needle, another landmark, was mentioned by Waltz, too.

Mystics as well as the Apache insist that the entire area is cursed. Perhaps those who catch treasure hunting fever become frenzied and obsessed and the curse lies in developing an addiction. Or perhaps the place really is evil.

Some feel Waltz invented the whole story to cover up a theft. Many years earlier, another legendary treasure of gold was rumored to have been hidden in the area by the Jesuits. The order arrived in the area about 1692 from Spain. They were sent to convert the native Apache to Christianity. However, the missionaries soon turned to mining instead. The mysterious religious cult was recalled by the King of Spain when he heard news of this turn of events.

The renegade Jesuits reputedly hid priceless religious artifacts as well as

the hoarded gold, probably with the intent to return for it later. The Jesuits were also accused of booby trapping some of the mine shafts. Many who began to look for the gold disappeared. A history of mysterious deaths and tragedies began to be connected with the Superstition Mountains. Hand prints in black paint can be found on rock faces. These are warning signs left by the Apache. Prehistoric petroglyphs are etched and painted in caves and on rocks. These relay messages from those who wandered in the area in centuries past.

The mountain range is composed of volcanic peaks estimated to be about 29 million years old by geologists. The desert climate tends to keep vegetation sparse in the area. Superstition Mountain itself reaches an elevation of 5,024 feet and the designated wilderness area is public land composed of about 160,000 acres. The whole mood of the place is one of mystery and unique beauty. Perhaps that is the true treasure it holds.

Today the fascination with treasure hunting continues. Despite so many deaths and disappearances, there is no shortage of those who are inspired to try a hand at treasure hunting. There are many who spend years of their lives wandering in the area, puzzling over the clues and different versions of Waltz's map. Some are followed and murdered by others who fear they might be closing in on the treasure. The ghosts of the victims of massacres have been sensed by some seekers.

Numerous videos about searching for the Lost Dutchman's treasure can be found on YouTube and The History Channel has dedicated a whole series to the topic. Many books and articles are available for the curious, as well as guides for those who would like to give treasure hunting a try.

Some acquaintances considered Jacob Waltz to be a pleasant and affable gentleman. Others who knew him described him as a monster.

—MARINA BRYONY

A Spell to Win Love

an excerpt from Charles Leland's
Aradia: Gospel of the Witches

WHEN A WIZARD, a worshipper of Diana, one who worships the Moon, desires the love of a woman, he can change her into the form of a dog, when she, forgetting who she is, and all things besides, will at once come to his house, and there, when by him, take on again her natural form and remain with him. And when it is time for her to depart, she will again become a dog and go home, where she will turn into a girl. And she will remember nothing of what has taken place, or at least but little or mere fragments, which will seem as a con-fused dream. And she will take the form of a dog because Diana has ever a dog by her side.

And this is the spell to be repeated by him who would bring a love to his home.[1]

Today is Friday, and I wish to rise very early, not having been able to sleep all night, having seen a very beautiful girl, the daughter of a rich lord, whom I dare not hope to win. Were she poor, I could gain her with money; but as she is rich, I have no hope to do so. (Therefore will I conjure Diana to aid me.)

---

1 The beginning of this spell seems to be merely a prose introduction explaining the nature of the ceremony.

Scongiurazione a Diana

Diana, bella Diana!
Che tanto bella e buona siei,
E tanto ti é piacere
Ti ho fatto,
Anche a te di fare al amore,
Dunque spero che anche in questa cosa
Tu mi voglia aiutare,
E se tu vorrai
Tutto tu potrai,
Se questa grazia mi vorrai fare:
Chiamerai tua figlia Aradia,
Al letto della bella fanciulla
La mandera Aradia,
La fanciulla in una canina convertira,
Alla camera mia la mandera,
Ma entrata in camera mia,
Non sarà più una canina,
Ma tornerà una bella fanciulla,
Bella cane era prima,
E cosi potrò fare al amore
A mio piacimento,
Come a me piacera.
Quando mi saro divertito
A mi piacere dirò.
"Per volere della Fata Diana,
E di sua figlia Aradia,
Torna una canina
Come tu eri prima!"

Invocation to Diana

Diana, beautiful Diana!
Who art indeed as good as beautiful,
By all the worship I have given thee,
And all the joy of love which thou hast known,
I do implore thee aid me in my love!
What thou wilt 'tis true
Thou canst ever do:
And if the grace I seek thou'lt grant to me,
Then call, I pray, thy daughter Aradia,
And send her to the bedside of the girl,
And give that girl the likeness of a dog,
And make her then come to me in my room,
But when she once has entered it, I pray
That she may reassume her human form,
As beautiful as e'er she was before,
And may I then make love to her until
Our souls with joy are fully satisfied.
Then by the aid of the great Fairy Queen
And of her daughter, fair Aradia,
May she be turned into a dog again,
And then to human form as once before!

Thus it will come to pass that the girl as a dog will return to her home unseen and unsuspected, for thus will it be effected by Aradia; and the girl will think it is all a dream, because she will have been enchanted by Aradia.

Aradia: Gospel of the Witches is available at TheWitchesAlmanac.com/products/aradia-or-the-gospel-of-the-witches

⚜ Looking Back ⚜

light a candle

TONIGHT create total darkness, then light a candle. To fully appreciate the experience and honor the act in the proper way, you might recite a very old chant:

Lord of fury, Lord of flame,
Smite the darkness with thy name.

Uta, Shamash, Baal, Rakashih, Ra, Mithra, Apollo, Lucifer... any one of a number of the Gods of light can be acknowledged. Murmur his name as you strike a match and, in one action, touch the flame to the candlewick.

Study the flame now as it sways to reveal your breath and the air currents in the room. It is easy to understand why the element of Fire was venerated by the ancients. You may know a feeling of curious contentment as you gaze steadily at the bright light before you.

Candles were used in religious rites as early as 3000 B.C. And they retained their sacred nature, for it was not until the Middle Ages that the wax candle came into general use as a means of illumination in the household.

In Witchcraft and ceremonial magic, lighting a candle is a usual prelude to the magic experience. The practical

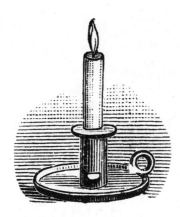

reason underlying the ritual is the need to concentrate psychic energy; the flame serves as a focal point. Beeswax candles formed by your own hand in any color you feel appropriate is the rule of witches. The ceremonial magician, however, follows a stricter path. The candles must be made by the practitioner from virgin wax (that taken from bees having made it for the first time), according to the *Key of Solomon*. The color of the wax is of vital importance and must correspond to the planet under whose aegis the rite will be performed.

> Sun—Gold or Yellow
> Moon—Silver or White
> Mars—Red
> Mercury—Mixed or Purple
> Jupiter—Blue
> Venus—Green
> Saturn—Black

Some occult traditions required that the candle be anointed with oil, wrapped in parchment and buried in the earth (wick pointing to the north) for an interval of a Moon phase prior to the rite.

It is fortunate that beeswax candles cannot only burn best but are the easiest to make. The requirements are simple: a room at an 80° temperature, a sharp knife and a smooth board on which to roll and cut. Round wicks and the solid or honeycombed sheets of colored beeswax are easily available by mail from the candle supply houses.

Candle spells are many. A most effective means of summoning is recorded in Old English folklore. Thrust two common pins through a lighted candle's wick to form a "T" and slowly chant:

> *It's not this candle alone I stick,*
> *but...'s heart I mean to prick.*
> *Whether asleep or awaken be,*
> *I summon his spirit to come to me.*

When the flame has burned down to the crossed pins, the person desired will appear in person or in a dream.

Moon Cycles

A New Moon rises with the Sun,
Her waxing half at midday shows,
The Full Moon climbs at sunset hour,
And waning half the midnight knows.

NEW	2024	FULL	NEW	2025	FULL
Jan. 11		Jan. 25			Jan. 13
Feb. 9		Feb. 24	Jan. 29		Feb. 12
Mar. 10		Mar. 25	Feb. 27		Mar. 14
Apr. 8		Apr. 23	Mar. 29		Apr. 12
May 7		May 23	Apr. 27		May 12
June 6		June 21	May 26		June 11
July 5		July 21	June 25		July 10
Aug. 4		Aug. 19	July 24		Aug. 9
Sept. 2		Sept. 17	Aug. 23		Sept. 7
Oct. 2		Oct. 17	Sept. 21		Oct. 6
Nov. 1		Nov. 15	Oct. 21		Nov. 5
Dec. 1		Dec. 15	Nov. 20		Dec. 4
Dec. 30*			Dec. 19		

*A rare second New Moon in a single month is called a "Black Moon."
**A rare second Full Moon in a single month is called a "Blue Moon."

Life takes on added dimension when you match your activities to the waxing and waning of the Moon. Observe the sequence of her phases to learn the wisdom of constant change within complete certainty.

Dates are for Eastern Standard and Daylight Time.

presage

by Dikki-Jo Mullen

ARIES, 2023–PISCES, 2024

THE EARTH is the theme of this year's *Witches' Almanac.* During these times caring for and understanding our home planet is an important priority for all. Perhaps this is especially true of those who follow the Old Ways. The spirituality sections of Presage this year include Peru's Nazca zodiac signs, adapted from the mysterious and ancient sky charts traced on the desert floor. The idea is to share the helpful spiritual insights the Nazca signs offer.

Pluto hovers on the Capricorn-Aquarius cusp all year. Astrologers have been calling this the most anticipated and influential astrological transit of the decade. Pluto will enter Aquarius on January 21, 2024 where it will remain for 20 years, until January 20 of 2044. The Presage forecasts factor in this profound celestial shift influence upon each zodiac sign. Transformation, endings and new beginnings are what Pluto, identified with the mythological God of the underworld,

is all about. Globally, Aquarian issues, including politics, social conditions, air, the space program, technology and science, will be highlighted.

Saturn and Neptune will transit Pisces all year. The water, mysticism, welfare of the disadvantaged as well as the uses for chemicals and medicines will be important concerns. Jupiter enters Taurus on May 16, 2023 where it will remain through the end of the year. This affects finances and the value of property.

Consult the forecast for your Sun sign, that's the well known, familiar birth sign, to understand how you can best shine during this significant time of personal and planetary change. The forecast for your Moon sign applies to processing memories, emotions and family situations. See the forecast for your ascendant (rising sign) to understand how the times to come will affect your appearance and personality, revealing how the rest of the world will view you. Here begins Presage.

ASTROLOGICAL KEYS

Signs of the Zodiac
Channels of Expression

ARIES: fiery, pioneering, competitive
TAURUS: earthy, stable, practical
GEMINI: dual, lively, versatile
CANCER: protective, traditional
LEO: dramatic, flamboyant, warm
VIRGO: conscientious, analytical
LIBRA: refined, fair, sociable
SCORPIO: intense, secretive, ambitious
SAGITTARIUS: friendly, expansive
CAPRICORN: cautious, materialistic
AQUARIUS: inquisitive, unpredictable
PISCES: responsive, dependent, fanciful

Elements
FIRE: Aries, Leo, Sagittarius
EARTH: Taurus, Virgo, Capricorn
AIR: Gemini, Libra, Aquarius
WATER: Cancer, Scorpio, Pisces

Qualities

CARDINAL	FIXED	MUTABLE
Aries	Taurus	Gemini
Cancer	Leo	Virgo
Libra	Scorpio	Sagittarius
Capricorn	Aquarius	Pisces

CARDINAL signs mark the beginning of each new season — active.
FIXED signs represent the season at its height — steadfast.
MUTABLE signs herald a change of season — variable.

Celestial Bodies
Generating Energy of the Cosmos

Sun: birth sign, ego, identity
Moon: emotions, memories, personality
Mercury: communication, intellect, skills
Venus: love, pleasures, the fine arts
Mars: energy, challenges, sports
Jupiter: expansion, religion, happiness
Saturn: responsibility, maturity, realities
Uranus: originality, science, progress
Neptune: dreams, illusions, inspiration
Pluto: rebirth, renewal, resources

Glossary of Aspects

Conjunction: two planets within the same sign or less than 10 degrees apart, favorable or unfavorable according to the nature of the planets.

Sextile: a pleasant, harmonious aspect occurring when two planets are two signs or 60 degrees apart.

Square: a major negative effect resulting when planets are three signs from one another or 90 degrees apart.

Trine: planets four signs or 120 degrees apart, forming a positive and favorable influence.

Quincunx: planets are 150 degrees or about 5 signs apart. The hand of fate is at work and unique challenges can develop. Sometimes a karmic situation emerges.

Opposition: a six-sign or 180° separation of planets generating positive or negative forces depending on the planets involved.

The Houses — *Twelve Areas of Life*

1st house: appearance, image, identity
2nd house: money, possessions, tools
3rd house: communications, siblings
4th house: family, domesticity, security
5th house: romance, creativity, children
6th house: daily routine, service, health

7th house: marriage, partnerships, union
8th house: passion, death, rebirth, soul
9th house: travel, philosophy, education
10th house: fame, achievement, mastery
11th house: goals, friends, high hopes
12th house: sacrifice, solitude, privacy

Eclipses

Elements of surprise, odd weather patterns, change and growth are linked to eclipses. Those with a birthday within three days of an eclipse can expect some shifts in the status quo. There will be four partial eclipses this year.

April, 20 2023—New Moon—partial solar eclipse in Aries, North Node
May 5, 2023—Full Moon—partial lunar eclipse in Scorpio, South Node
October 14, 2023—New Moon—partial solar eclipse in Libra, South Node
October 28, 2023—Full Moon—partial lunar eclipse in Taurus, North Node

A total eclipse is more influential than a partial. The eclipses conjunct the Moon's North Node are thought to be more favorable than those conjunct the South Node.

Retrograde Planetary Motion

Retrogrades promise a change of pace, different paths and perspectives.

Mercury Retrograde

Impacts technology, travel and communication. Those who have been out of touch return. Revise, review and tread familiar paths. Affected: Gemini and Virgo

April 21, 2023–May 15, 2023
in Taurus
August 24, 2023–September 16, 2023
in Virgo
December 13, 2023–January 2, 2024
in Sagittarius and Capricorn

Venus Retrograde

Venus retrograde influences art, finances, and love. Affected: Taurus and Libra

July 23, 2023–September 4, 2023 in Leo

Mars Retrograde

The military, sports, and heavy industry are impacted. Affected: Aries and Scorpio. There will not be a Mars retrograde this year.

Jupiter Retrograde

Large animals, speculation, education, and religion are impacted. Affected: Sagittarius and Pisces

September 4, 2023–December 31, 2023
in Taurus

Saturn Retrograde

Elderly people, the disadvantaged, employment and natural resources are linked to Saturn. Affected: Capricorn and Aquarius

June 18, 2023–November 4, 2023
in Pisces.

Uranus Retrograde

Inventions, science, electronics, revolutionaries and extreme weather relate to Uranus retrograde. Affected: Aquarius

August 29, 2023–January 27, 2024
in Taurus

Neptune Retrograde

Water, aquatic creatures, chemicals, spiritual forces and psychic phenomena are impacted by this retrograde. Affected: Pisces

July 1, 2023–December 6, 2023
in Pisces

Pluto Retrograde

Ecology, espionage, birth and death rates, nuclear power and mysteries relate to Pluto retrograde. Affected: Scorpio

May 2, 2023–October 11, 2023
in Capricorn and Aquarius

ARIES

March 20–April 19

Spring 2023–Spring 2024 for those
born under the sign of the Ram

With dynamic Mars as the ruler, Aries is all about action. Physical activity and exercise are always beneficial to you. The pioneering spirit of this first sign of the zodiac accents starting new ventures. Participate in all that is innovative and fresh. Follow through with completion though. Focus on finishing a project before moving on to the next new thing, otherwise your efforts and resources could be squandered. Shortcuts appeal to you. Aries prefers to get to the point and arrive quickly. Your always scant patience disappears completely when situations are repetitive and too long lasting. You thrive when encountering competition and challenges.

Springtime begins with a rush of plans, conversations and ideas. Mercury races through your birth sign from the Vernal Equinox through April 2. In mid-April a social event or a creative idea generates extra income. The solar eclipse on April 20 brings a game changer regarding financial situations. The first three weeks of May finds Mars making a stir concerning your home life. On May Eve prepare a house blessing and make arrangements to complete repairs. Late May–June 4 a Venus influences smooths away tensions with a relative. It's time for decorating, entertaining, or painting your home. The remainder of June is all about pleasure. Both Venus and Mars will glide through your sector of romance, leisure and hobbies. At the Summer Solstice bless a love token to delight your nearest and dearest. July finds Saturn retrograde. Vulnerabilities and secret worries must be addressed. Try positive affirmations or study something new to overcome a spell of depression. At Lammas gather fresh and healthy fruits, vegetables and grains for the early harvest meal. July 10–August 27 Mars affects your health sector. Practice moderation. Take time for breaks if daily life seems especially tiring or stressful. Rest, relax and rejuvenate.

Early September brings a Mars opposition to your Sun. Others can be more assertive and competitive than usual. A bit of humor can diffuse an impending confrontation. Focus on cooperation and balance through the Autumnal Equinox. The Full Moon in your birth sign on September 29 can bring a situation out into the open. October 5–21 others offer suggestions and approach you with ideas and plans. Mercury's influence then presents a broader view point. October 22–31 shifts several transits, including the Sun, to your 8th house. Paranormal activity intensifies. Friendly spirits hover nearby. Visiting a museum or antique shoppe offers glimpses into other dimensions. At All Hallows consider a costume featuring a character from a favorite detective story.

In early November Saturn changes direction, bringing renewed hope and optimism. On November 8 Venus enters your relationship sector. Invitations arrive. Prepare for a whirlwind of social events. Someone close to you reveals new talents. During December Mars joins the Sun in your 9th house. Imported items or foreign travel can pique your interest. An international theme is a good choice for a holiday celebration. On December 13 Mercury turns retrograde near your midheaven. This trend underscores repeating patterns affecting your career. Look to the past to understand the present. A colleague can be at the center of some controversy.

The Winter Solstice favors a quiet, contemplative mood. On the longest of nights enjoy a cup of hot chocolate and read a seasonal poem or hum holiday tunes. December 23–January 13 Mercury trines your Sun. Be observant and alert. Events bring a new perspective. The last half of January accents your career sector. An influential person will appreciate your efforts. By Candlemas an opportunity appears. Dedicate a red candle for action at a sacred rite on February 1–2.

On February 5 Mercury joins the Sun in your 11th house. Humanitarian issues assume new significance throughout mid-February. The New Moon on February 9 features ecology or social unrest. The end of February through March 11 finds you feeling connected to a new circle of associates. From March 12 through Winter's end Venus will join Saturn and Neptune in your sector of charity and sacrifice. It's a good time to accept a volunteer position or to perform random acts of kindness.

HEALTH

Patience is important when working toward better health. Jupiter, the celestial healer, will conjoin your Sun from the Vernal Equinox through May 15. This is a time when health goals can be reached. The New Moon in Aries on March 21, 2023 coincides with the Vernal Equinox. This is a wonderful time to write a wish list of your health goals and needs for the year to come.

LOVE

From June 5 to October 8 Venus makes a long transit through your 5th house of romance, with a rare Venus retrograde cycle in the mix. A second chance with a lost love can arise then, or a new attraction that has a karmic or past life angle can develop. The Full Moons on September 29, 2023 and January 25, 2024 can bring passionate interludes followed by declarations of true love.

SPIRITUALITY

Aries, your Nazca zodiac sign is the Dog. Spiritual blessings come to you through friendships. A special canine companion can be a source of spiritual comfort.

FINANCE

Eclipses on April 20 and October 28, affect your financial sector this year. A new source of income could replace an old one. Uranus is in the eclipse mix too, pointing to sudden developments. Live within your means, budget carefully. After December 31 when Jupiter turns direct in your 2nd house of money, the financial picture should move into a more promising phase.

TAURUS
April 20–May 20
Spring 2023–Spring 2024 for those
born under the sign of the Bull

Taurus comes from a place of stability and determination. This almost always allows the Bull to acquire whatever is desired. Ruled by Venus, Taurus is attracted to quality, beauty and luxury. Many of the most successful gardeners are born with this practical Earth sign. There is a genuine connection with plants, trees and flowers. Surprise upsets in the daily schedule won't be appreciated.

The Vernal Equinox is ushered in gently with Venus in your birth sign. This favorable influence lasts through April 10. You feel appreciated by family and coworkers alike. An artistic venture proceeds well. A solar eclipse on April 20 brings news of impending changes. Welcome a fresh situation. Breaking away from a rut and welcoming an opportunity to grow can change the direction of your life now. Mercury is retrograde in your 1st house April 21–May 15. Draw upon experiences. Reconnect with social and professional contacts from the past to help you prepare for the times ahead. Late May through July 9 Mars influences your home and family sector. At the Summer Solstice prepare a house blessing or make some Feng Shui style adjustments in home décor. A remodeling or repair project might require attention. A volatile

family situation is likely. Compromise to diffuse hurt feelings or anger. A strong Venus transit will come into play during mid-July and August. This accents family bonds and loyalties. At Lammas include heirloom china or other decorative keepsakes on a table of seasonal breads and fruits. Retrograde Venus turns direct on September 4 and a misunderstanding heals making a problematic or uncomfortable issue become a memory.

As September begins Mars affects your health sector. Address fitness and wellness goals. At the Autumnal Equinox bless a talisman for health. Explore the concept of self care. A sage smudge of your home or workplace to welcome the new season would be refreshing. On October 9 Venus begins a transit through your 5th house. There can be pride and happiness regarding a child's accomplishments and progress. This celestial influence also favors love, hobbies and recreational pursuits. Overall the Autumn days will be positive and uplifting, assuming a bright and colorful hue. All Hallows Eve arrives with the Sun, Mercury and Mars in opposition to your Sun. Let others make plans and accept invitations. Consider a partner's ideas and suggestions when selecting a Halloween costume.

November begins with Saturn hovering on the cusp of your 11th house. This ushers in serious considerations about both your social circle and a long-range goal. If you have outgrown a friendship it might be time to create some distance. A new direction can be worth exploring if you feel blocked. November 10–30 Mercury impacts the 8th house. This brings mysterious facts to the surface.

Insights are presented. Heed synchronicities, omens and coincidences. They can include subtle guidance sent by a helpful spirit guide.

On December 2 Mercury begins a favorable transit which sets the pace until the Winter Solstice. Opportunities to travel or enroll in an educational program can be presented. Explore these possibilities. They might pave the way for you to reach a professional or personal goal. The specifics will become apparent by December 22. Dedicate Winter Solstice observances to honoring time and seeking wisdom. On December 31 Jupiter completes its retrograde and moves forward in Taurus.

As 2024 begins the pace of your life picks up. This promising influence affects you throughout the remainder of the Winter season. A talent can emerge or other potentials surface. The week of the New Moon on January 11 reveals details. Venus trines your Sun January 23–February 15. Both social and financial prospects are excellent. Combine business with pleasure. A friendly co-worker does you a favor. Enjoyable gatherings brighten the time from Candlemas through Valentine's Day.

The last two weeks of February can be intense and demanding. Mars crosses your midheaven and squares your Sun. Expect to extend effort to fulfill an obligation or complete a project. Use diplomacy to diffuse a confrontation with a forceful competitor. March 1–11 brings insights into concerns. From March 12 through Winter's end Venus, Saturn and the Sun gather in your 11th house. Your perspective brightens. Helpful friends will offer encouragement.

HEALTH

On May 17 benevolent Jupiter, the heavenly healer, enters Taurus and remains in your sign for the rest of the year. This is an influence which encourages recovery from health conditions and points to a higher level of overall well-being. Because Jupiter relates to growth and expansion, do control your weight though. A sensible diet is essential this year.

LOVE

Venus, the love goddess among the planets, will be retrograde July 23–September 4. An old flame rekindles. History repeats itself. The retrograde cycle shows a need to postpone any changes in the relationship status. Good months for love are April, October and February.

SPIRITUALITY

In the Nazca zodiac Taurus becomes the sign of the Hand. The outreach and touch of the powerful sky gods and the weather elements is the message of the Hand. The lunar eclipses on May 5 and October 28 promise spiritual experiences. Full Moon circles or meditation and rituals at those times can offer messages from angels and spirit guides.

FINANCE

The solar eclipse on April 20 hints at an economic twist affecting personal finances. However, the Winter brings promising changes with Jupiter and Uranus moving forward in Taurus. This favorable influence will be strongest from January 27 through March 19.

GEMINI
May 21 – June 20

Spring 2023 – Spring 2024 for those
born under the sign of the Twins

An Air sign, Gemini is like the wind. Constantly in motion while voicing ideas and thoughts you gather diverse parts into a unique whole. Ruled by Mercury, the planet of communication and intellect, the symbol of the Twins suggests mediation. Gemini can be a translator, sharing through language, expressions of both the body and soul with gestures, writings and conversation. Always inquisitive, you love to explore and take short journeys.

The Vernal Equinox arrives with Mars in conjunction with your Sun. March 20 – 24 your energy level will be high; complete a project with aplomb. March 25 – April 10 your sector of hopes and friendships is highlighted. Friends include you in discussions about plans for the future. It's an optimal time to become more active in groups and organizations. From April 11 to May 6 Venus transits Gemini. Relationships strengthen, business and pleasure combine and life offers much to enjoy. Share May Eve festivities with congenial companions. During the last three weeks of May to June 10 Mercury, Jupiter and Uranus affect your 12th house. A reserved reverie prevails. You will cherish quiet moments to process private thoughts and feelings. June 11 – 26 Mercury races through your first house. Quick solutions arise enabling you to complete work ahead of schedule. At the Summer Solstice prepare a charm for travel.

By mid-July Mars will affect your home life. A change of residence is possible. Be patient if a relative is argumentative. At Lammas prepare a house blessing. Explore family history and hereditary factors during August. This will help you to cherish and understand your roots. The Full Moon on August 30 brings visibility to your professional status. Make the most of a chance to display your stellar skills and shine.

Mercury completes its retrograde on September 16. Uncertainty and tension can be resolved regarding family dynamics by the Autumnal Equinox. Late September through October 22 brings favorable influences from Mars and the Sun in your sector of love and leisure. Enjoy a new hobby or flirtation. Select wholesome snacks at All Hallows and fashion harvest style decorations from natural materials. A scarecrow would be a good costume choice.

Saturn changes direction in your 10th house of career during the first week of November. You are ready to seek a promotion or new challenge at work; a past effort is rewarded. Mars moves in to oppose your Sun by the end of November. The Full Moon in Gemini on November 27 clarifies the specifics. A competitive element develops during late November and December. Keep rivalry good natured and the challenges presented can become an asset. At the Winter Solstice a mystical mood prevails and spiritual presences hover nearby. Design a ritual emphasizing peace during the longest of nights. On December 31 Jupiter changes direction in your 12th house. Help comes from an unexpected source; there is a benevolent angelic presence.

January begins with Mercury and Venus in your 7th house. Others offer suggestions and make plans. Compromise, cooperate. Early 2024 is a time when employing teamwork enables goals to be reached. The Full Moon on January 25 brings a helpful exchange of ideas during a conference. Candlemas finds five planets in earth signs. Light candles to acknowledge ecological issues as well as prosperity concerns. During February Pluto moves forward, applying to a favorable trine aspect to your Sun. It is easier to resolve and understand a challenging past experience. Suddenly you will realize that things really do happen for a reason. When Mercury changes signs on February 5 you will enjoy a new sense of clarity and divine guidance.

From mid-February through Winter's end an upbeat Mars trend sets the pace. Your energy and motivation are high, allowing you to accomplish much. During March the Sun and Venus will cross your midheaven. Professional associates will become more friendly and thoughtful. Develop creative ideas March 12–19.

HEALTH
On May 5 an eclipse affects your 6th house of health and diet. Embrace more wholesome lifestyles choices then, and health can improve during Spring and Summer. April 3–June 10 a very long Mercury transit in your 12th house accents the mind-body connection. Foster a positive mental outlook, perhaps including meditation and positive affirmations to enhance wellness,

LOVE
April 11–May 6 brings a promising Venus transit. Cultivate social opportunities or nurture an existing relationship then. Offer a pretty basket or bouquet on May Day to one whom you fancy. The eclipse on October 14 profoundly affects your love sector. There can be a significant romantic experience near that time. November 8–December 4 brings celestial patterns which favor romance. Intellectual stimulation is always important to you in a potential love match. Seek happiness with a special someone whose wit intrigues you.

SPIRITUALITY
In the Nazca zodiac Gemini's sign is the Tree. Knowledge of both good and evil is linked to tree symbolism, making it an illustration of spiritual duality. The multifaceted aspects of faith will be appealing. You would appreciate finding both light and darkness within the divinity.

FINANCE
Throughout this entire year a square from Saturn to your Sun accents ambition and supports devotion to a steady work ethic, bringing solid rewards. You will feel driven to achieve greater affluence. Patience and careful budgeting will bring rewards in time, but do avoid excessive risks this year. June favors opportunities to earn extra money while an investment, insurance settlement or inheritance could be lucrative in January or February.

CANCER
June 21–July 22
Spring 2023–Spring 2024 for those
born under the sign of the Crab

This sensitive Water sign operates from an emotional perspective. Memories, home and family ties are always significant. The introspective Crab cherishes privacy. Just as a crab is protected by its shell, Cancerians will maintain barriers and boundaries as a defense against intrusion. Ruled by the Moon, you are changeable and receptive. Always remain aware of how your surroundings and associates are influencing you. Avoid negativity. Just as the Moon reflects sunlight, you will reflect the influences of your environment. Collectibles, keepsakes and fine cuisine are appreciated by the sentimental Crab.

At the Vernal Equinox Mercury creates a stir in your career sector. Meetings and new developments are significant. On March 25 Mars enters Cancer. This sets a busy pace until early June. You will become more assertive, speaking out about annoying situations. Much can be accomplished if you approach making changes with the right amount of humor and patience. Your attitude is competitive near May Eve. Enjoy exercise, maybe dancing around a Maypole. Dedicate a crystal to help in overcoming anger and stress. During the last three weeks of May Venus will conjoin your Sun. Focus on creative projects, build rapport in relationships. You can add beauty to your life. Your 12th house of compassion and sacrifice is highlighted during June. You will offer charity and assistance to an animal, child or an elderly person in need.

At the Summer Solstice focus on healing rituals. Celestial patterns favor travel during July. The Full Moon on July 3 brings an intriguing invitation. A change of scene would be refreshing. Consider a waterfront journey/vacation. July 9–late August Mars transits your 3rd house. Neighborhood dynamics or a sibling relationship can be tense. Examine options and gather information to resolve conflicts. The New Moon on July 17 favors self analysis. "Know thyself" as the Oracle of Delphi advised. Early August is busy. Multitasking leads to accomplishment. Prepare a wholesome meal and dedicate a ritual to health and peace at Lammas. During August retrograde Venus blesses your finances. A lucrative income opportunity arises. Try creative expression of salable job skills. A friend provides valuable financial advice.

September finds Mars stirring your sector of family and residence. A new home or household renovation and repairs can be considered. At the Autumnal Equinox do a house blessing. Feng shui techniques can be helpful. Early October brings an interest in novelty. The unfamiliar is alluring. The eclipse on October 14 brings insights regarding history and heritage. Social connections bring surprises at the October 28 eclipse. An opportunity to network with a new organization near All Hallows is worth considering. Add a gadget, flashing lights or a noisemaker to Halloween décor. November 1–9 favorable influences between Mercury and Neptune emphasize psychic perception. Take note of and interpret a vivid dream. The first three weeks of November find Mars and the Sun affecting your love and leisure sector. Enjoy a favorite hobby, sports or the pursuit of romance. The end of November favors releasing stress. Take time to meditate and relax.

December 4–30 Venus brings a gracious influence. A child's accomplishments can be a source of joy. This also favors artistic interests. At the Winter Solstice enjoy seasonal musicals or theatrical productions. Entertain and decorating to celebrate the holiday season. December 31–January 4 both Mercury and Jupiter complete retrograde cycles. Animal companions bring joy. Consider adopting a new pet. From early January through February 12 Mars will oppose your Sun. Partnerships and team work are a focus. Keep rivalry constructive and good humored. Make a competitor an ally at the New Moon on January 11.

At Candlemas illuminate candles with multiple wicks symbolizing cooperation and unity. During February several transits affect your sector of service and organization. Budget time and resources. Keep promises. Others rely on you. The Full Moon on February 24 brings the clearing of a conundrum. Leap Day, February 29, brings benevolent water sign influences. Burdens lighten. The month ends with a pleasant surprise. March 1–10 Mercury and Saturn harmonize in your 9th house. This facilitates travel and study. Winter ends on an idealistic note. Favorable Venus and Neptune influences suggest spiritual awakening. Angelic forces are in evidence.

HEALTH

On May 17 Jupiter changes sings, moving into a favorable sextile aspect to your Sun which lasts through the Winter. Wellness efforts will progress nicely during this time period. The axiom "your food should be your medicine and your medicine should be your food" especially applies now.

LOVE

The eclipse on May 5 profoundly impacts your sector of romance. Cultivate love connections which seem happy and promising at that time. Early June, mid-December and mid-March bring favorable Venus transits to highlight love prospects then. Release connections which have been turbulent in the past.

SPIRITUALITY

In the Nazca zodiac Cancer's sign becomes the Lizard. Immortality and shapeshifting are the gifts brought by the graceful and elusive lizard. Spiritual insights can come through past life studies as well as adapting to changing trends. Spiritual awakening can come through taking note of and interpreting dreams and meditations near the Full Moon on August 30 and again at the New Moon on March 10.

FINANCE

A very long Venus transit in your 2nd house of money spans June 5–October 8. This whole cycle points to a time when the money situation gradually becomes more promising. You are able to afford a long desired item.

LEO

July 23–August 22
Spring 2023–Spring 2024 for those
born under the sign of the Lion

With your natural nobility and dignity, Leo, combined with your lively disposition, you bring a warm and bright sparkle wherever you go. Like the Sun, your ruler, you act as a catalyst for growth too. Courageous and entertaining, you have a playful side. You enjoy games, parties and are a romantic at heart.

The Vernal Equinox finds serious Saturn just crossing the cusp of your 8th house. There is a mystery to solve regarding the well-being of a loved one. By March 26 Mercury and Jupiter favor your sector of higher thought. New information brings sudden insights, answering important questions. April 1–11 Venus affects your status and recognition. Colleagues are friendly and helpful. During the last part of April through May Eve Mars shadows your 12th house. You will crave some quiet time and may withdraw from a pressing social situation. Your natural flamboyance resurfaces in early May. This can involve taking pleasure in being active with a charity or a volunteer position. Offer spiritual healing and advice to help those less fortunate on May Day. May 2–17 you will long to wander and explore. A Jupiter influence favors widening horizons. The eclipse on May 5 hints at unexpected developments in your job.

You attract attention and your visibility is great during May. On May 20 Mars enters your birth sign, bringing an intense peak of energy which lasts through July 9. You will be motivated to stand up for what is most important. Maintain a comfortable pace and this time span can be very productive. The Summer Solstice is dynamic. Exercise or playing a game can be exhilarating. You will deepen connections to the Old Ways.

July 10–29 Mercury dashes through your 1st house. Expect a burst of mental energy and much variety. This promises travel, exciting conversations and new projects unfolding simultaneously. During August Venus will be retrograde in Leo, bringing a chance to mend or renew heartfelt connections. At Lammastide reach out to make things right with a lost love. Analyze patterns regarding closest relationships during August. Express and strengthen true love near your birthday. An exceptionally lengthy Venus conjunction to your Sun prevails through October 8. This continues to prioritize romance as well as the expression of creative ideas. Plan a party to celebrate the Autumnal Equinox. Make seasonal decorations in fall colors and serve platters of beautiful pastries and sweets. Exchange a sentimental token with one you care for.

Mercury, the Sun and Mars meet in your 4th house of heritage and home during late October. You will invest serious effort into creating the ideal home and family life. A residential move might be appealing. At All Hallows resurrect vintage Halloween ornaments and costumes. Traditional decorations such as jack o' lanterns provide a cheery holiday setting.

November 1–9 a square from Mercury generates restlessness. It can be hard to concentrate. Take some breaks to avoid mental exhaustion. The last three weeks of November will shift the focus to your 5th house. An enjoyable avocation brightens the Autumn evenings. Expect a hint of romance too. December 1–22 Mercury joins Pluto in your health sector. Examine information pertaining to wellness. Your health habits or a chronic condition could impact well-being. Plan a warm and cozy celebration honoring the Winter Solstice. Dedicate a yule log to a wish for improved health in the times to come.

December 23–31 a Jupiter station squares your Sun. Balance excesses. It's easy to be a bit impractical if purchasing a luxury item or splurging in any way. January finds a Uranus influence prominent in your sector of career and recognition. There could be a sudden shift in the status quo affecting your profession. Adapt. Try innovation. The Full Moon on January 25 illuminates the specifics. By Candlemas Mercury, Venus and Mars will form a quincunx aspect to your Sun. Complete obligations, fulfill promises. Light plain white candles to symbolize cleanliness and simplicity. Throughout February others offer suggestions. Cooperate.

March 1–9 Mercury joins Saturn and Neptune in your 8th house of mysteries and secrets. Insights concerning the afterlife and spirit world arise. The New Moon on March 10 reveals much. During the last days of Winter a refreshing Mercury transit turns thoughts and conversations toward new possibilities including travel.

HEALTH

This year Pluto will gradually exit your health sector where it has hovered for many years. New health care practitioners and self care practices become a part of your path to improved vitality. This culminates during the mid to late Winter months.

LOVE

June–October a love attachment goes through several stages. There can be a sense of fated and karmic factors being at work. Attune to how a relationship is affecting your life overall to make the best decision. January brings a nurturing and enjoyable cycle in love.

SPIRITUALITY

Leo is symbolized by the Iguana in the spiritual Nazca zodiac. Sacred fire, your element, and your ruler, the Sun, are thought to have come from the Iguana. Iguanas are credited with generating lightning, hail, illumination, energy, and inspiration for spiritual awakening. Ignite incense and sacred fires for meditation when the Moon is full in Fire signs (June 3, September 29 and January 25). These will be times when spiritual truths can be revealed.

FINANCE

Two eclipses this year, on April 20 and October 28, point to changes in your profession. It is essential that you attune to current needs and trends. The Springtime, March 21–May 15, brings a positive and lucky influence from Jupiter. Good financial opportunities are present then.

VIRGO
August 23–September 22
Spring 2023–Spring 2024 for those
born under the sign of the Virgin

"Practical adaptability" perfectly describes earthy, Mercury-ruled Virgo. Perfectly is the key word. Seeking perfection in an imperfect world is the Virgo's quest. Responsible and efficient you are an incisive communicator. Dedication and quiet charm are highlighted by subtle wit. You are a helpful problem solver, adept at keeping the day's business on schedule. There is a deep affinity with small animals and reverence for nature's beauty.

From the Vernal Equinox through April 3 Mercury probes your 8th house. Consult Tarot cards or your pendulum. There is a mystery to solve. A connection with a spirit guide deepens. Mid-April is about culture and beauty, as Venus is influential. Visit an art gallery or enjoy music. A nostalgic and sentimental mood springs from retrograde Mercury for May Day. Place flowers in an antique vase or May basket to offer to friend. Mid-May to early June finds Venus favoring your 11th house. Your circle of acquaintances expands. It's a good time to network and interact. Others voice worthwhile ideas. The Summer Solstice accents charity projects. You might collect food and supplies for animals in need or find an opportunity to benefit disadvantaged persons by the end of June.

Mars transits Virgo from July 10 until August 26, The pattern is dynamic. Competition and the expectations of others propel you forward. Take shelter from the heat and pace yourself. Work or exercise can become demanding. Honor Lammas with sacred fire. Gaze into the flames and smoke and envision the harvest season to come. Mercury retrogrades back and forth near your Sun throughout August and September. Travel as well as study enriches your life. At the Autumnal Equinox review the ideas and opportunities which have been presented. Select an avenue to pursue further. October brings financial considerations to the forefront. The eclipse on October 14 can bring a new source of income or a shift affecting your salable job skills. Adapt, avoid financial risks during the weeks leading up to Halloween. Display colorful and cheerful seasonal decorations to bring magic to the daily grind. Include a laughing pumpkin.

November brings a favorable financial cycle. Monetary pressures can ease and work is more enjoyable from November 8 though December 4. A colleague's friendship and support is encouraging. During the Winter holiday season Mars will affect your home and family life. Compromise to maintain peace if a relative expresses frustrations. Take care of any repairs needed to make your dwelling as comfortable as possible. Examine your heritage for insights into family life. At the Winter Solstice a house blessing would be helpful, perhaps combining it with a family meeting and discussion. Make the occasion a celebration. Create a festive mood by serving a favorite dessert or hot mulled cider.

January 1–13 brings noise and nervous energy. Situations gradually become more settled following the New Moon on January 11. Add variety to routine and maintain good humor. During January Jupiter and Uranus complete retrograde cycles in your 9th house of higher thought. You will transcend and outgrow old attitudes and develop a broader perspective. Touring faraway places and exploring other cultures can be a tempting prospect by Candlemas. Dream of the warmer, brighter days to come while lighting silver or white candles at sunset on February 1–2. Mid-February brings Venus into your zone of love and pleasure. Share a favorite hobby or pastime with a congenial companion. February 17–March 11 brings a time of reverie. You will find peace through maintaining reserve and keeping your own counsel. Information about an associate surfaces which skews a relationship near the New Moon on March 10. During Winter's last days Saturn and the Sun bring clarity and truth regarding a close partnership. You will reflect on how a connection is affecting your own future. A crossroad is reached.

HEALTH

Pluto hovers near the cusp of your 6th house of health all year. This points to how health services and concerns which relate to humanity en masse will affect your personal well-being. Pluto's final sign change on January 21, 2024 can bring a transformative impact on your approach to health care. New medical professionals and innovative ideas can be selected. The Full Moon on August 1 foreshadows the specifics. The week of that lunation favors seeking information about health care needs and options.

LOVE

All year long Saturn and Neptune will oppose your Sun while transiting your sector of partnership. Seek a spiritual or creative focus in closest relationships. Pull away from anyone who might disappoint you with evasive or addictive behaviors. Fulfilling responsibilities and maintaining loyalty will be important. Enjoyable times in love connections are promised during good Venus transits October 9–November 7 and January 23–February 15. Prepare a special Valentine's Day outing or gift.

SPIRITUALITY

Virgo, the Spider is your symbol in the Nazca zodiac of Peru. Weave a web of connections. The Spider symbolizes links of deep passion and intimacy. Benevolent companions and the passage of time are honored by this sign. A Neptune opposition this year underscores spiritual examples and experiences which are brought into your life by others. Meditate on the Full Moon on August 30 for deeper spiritual awakening and awareness.

FINANCE

The financial expenses and needs of others can impact your own financial security this year. Approach assuming new financial obligations or entering into any agreements involving shared finances cautiously. The eclipse on October 14 brings a new twist on finances. Your hard work and efforts are rewarded by late Winter. That is when a lucky Jupiter influence promises financial improvement.

LIBRA
September 23–October 23
Spring 2023–Spring 2024 for those
born under the sign of the Scales

Peaceful and harmonious company appeal to this hospitable birth sign. You have a flair for putting others at ease. Your symbol, the Scales, illustrates the quest for balance. You try to always see both sides of situations. This often places you in the role of peacemaker or mediator. Libra is so anxious to do the right thing that "decision by indecision" frequently determines important outcomes. Appreciation for beauty and a passion for justice often feature prominently in Librans' lives.

The Vernal Equinox arrives amid controversy with a Mercury opposition. Others voice different ideas and it can be challenging to compromise. This influence is in effect until April 2. The Full Moon in Libra on April 6 reveals options which suggest a fair conflict resolution. The remainder of April through May 19 promises to be especially dynamic. Mars affects your midheaven, bringing competition and visibility. Your career motivation will be high and colleagues will seek your guidance. Dedicate May Eve to offering notes or tokens of appreciation to those you care for. Late May–June 4 Venus brightens your career sector. Friendship and goodwill as well as some extra income brighten your professional aspirations. Mid-June through the Summer Solstice a favorable Mercury influence in your 9th house piques your curiosity. Exploring a new topic of study or journeying to an unexplored location shifts your perspective. On the longest of days study a globe or map. Bless a beautiful seashell as a talisman for safe travels.

July brings celestial highlights from Venus. Long-term wishes and dreams are discussed with friends. Activities within an organization can play a role in this. Relationships deepen. By Lammas camaraderie is a source of valuable encouragement and support. Share a potluck-style feast to honor the early harvest. Throughout August you will feel responsibility for the vulnerable. Seek time to relax. On August 27 Mars enters Libra. The pace of life accelerates, remaining eventful throughout September. A new challenge or project exhilarates you. At the Autumnal Equinox reflect upon priorities in preparation for the new season to come. September 23–October 8 rewarding volunteer opportunities arise. The workload lessens when Mars leaves your sign on October 11. The solar eclipse at the New Moon on October 14 encourages leaving behind a situation which has grown stale or redundant. A change of job or residence can be appealing. The last half of October brings an increasing interest in boosting earning power and meeting financial obligations. At Halloween focus on a prosperity ritual. Explore how your job title can offer a clue for a clever costume idea.

Venus dances through your 1st house November 8–December 4. Your charisma level is strong; life is good. You are attracting positive situations regarding both love and money. Mercury affects your home and family sector during the 2nd and 3rd weeks of December. Visitors arrive, and an old acquaintance might reconnect. New technologies, perhaps including sound systems, televisions or computers, might be considered by the Winter Solstice. December 22–early January planets gather in your 3rd house. News involving a neighbor or sibling is brought to your attention. Transportation suddenly becomes a priority; a new vehicle might be needed.

Near the New Moon on January 11 important family or residential matters are a focus. Late January through February 4 brings mysteries and puzzles regarding the family tree into consideration. At Candlemas study your family's roots. Understanding heritage and inherited traits leads to valuable insights. Venus enters your 5th house of love and pleasure on February 16. This congenial trend sets an upbeat pace through March 11. A romantic interlude brings you solace and inspiration. March 12–19 a Mars trend adds fiery intensity to an attraction. One whom you admire shares your favorite hobby or pastime. This brings happiness as Winter ends.

HEALTH

All year long Saturn transits your health sector. Embrace preventative health measures. Extra sleep is a wonderful gift to give yourself if your vitality and energy levels are low. Others impact your health. Avoid those who drain your energy or engage in risky health practices. June 18–November 4, while Saturn is retrograde, examine your health history and habits for clues related to maintaining wellness.

LOVE

June 5–October 8 finds the celestial love goddess, Venus, passing through your 11th house of friendship and networking. Accept invitations from friends during this time. At an event you could connect with a new romantic prospect. Also a friendship could evolve into a closer connection. April 11–May 6, November 8–December 4 and February 16–March 11 are favorable for love.

SPIRITUALITY

In Peru's Nazca zodiac, Libra's spiritual guide is the Condor. A large and high flying black bird, Condor is seen as a messenger from the mountain Gods. Its presence exudes grace, dignity and idealism. Open air spaces, breezes and winds and the appearance of fallen feathers can relate to important spiritual awakenings from Condor. Collect feathers to add to your altar as spiritual talismans. The Libra Full Moon on April 6 as well as the solar eclipse at the New Moon on October 14 are times of potential spiritual significance.

FINANCE

From mid-May through the end of Winter Jupiter, the planet of luck and wealth, makes an interesting passage through your 8th house. This hints at unearned income. Money can come through an inheritance, insurance settlement, investment, or a gift. This year's eclipses in the Spring and Autumn can bring surprise twists to money matters. Be conservative. Avoid spending or making risky financial choices.

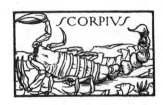

SCORPIO
October 24–November 21
Spring 2023–Spring 2024 for those
born under the sign of the Scorpion

Scorpio approaches life purposefully. You probe situations and circumstances, fulfilling a passion for depth. Your focus is on the mysteries of birth, the afterlife and the whole spectrum of possibilities in between. There is curiosity about the realms of magic and taboos too. Scorpio has a knack for transformation and reinvention. An inclination to spark social revolution or concentrate on research might be present. Science and finance are other areas of interest. Secrets of all kinds captivate this Pluto-ruled Water sign. Highly sensitive, you usually mask disappointments or hurt feelings.

The Vernal Equinox finds Venus in your relationship sector, a trend which sets the pace until April 10. A close partner expresses love and exhibits charm as well as talent. Dedicate May Eve to storytelling and poetry reading. The eclipse in Scorpio on May 5 ushers in a series of surprising upsets in the status quo. Adapt. Be receptive to change and all will be well in the end. A Mercury opposition in May and early June brings suggestions from others. Many lively discussions take place. June and early July find Mars impacting your career sector. A highly competitive mood prevails. Keep rivalry good natured and much can

be accomplished. All eyes are upon you at the Summer Solstice. Dedicate ritual observances to blessing your visibility and reputation. Confidently display what you're able to do and success is yours.

During the last half of July celestial patterns indicate possible distortions of the truth. Check facts. Don't exaggerate. Consider the details carefully if making promises or signing contracts. At Lammastide divination with the Tarot or pendulum brings clarity. Your 11th house is highlighted during August. A new project or goal is presented which could impact the trajectory of your life. September is about seeking peace. At the Autumnal Equinox a solitary stroll or meditation session can help with stress release. As September ends lend a helping hand to someone who is down on their luck. Pay it forward. A charitable gesture from you is appreciated. The favor will be rewarded in the future.

As October begins there is an urge to detach from negative drama. When Mars enters your birth sign on October 12 everything changes. You'll experience a surge of energy and motivation. Controversy, exercise and leadership roles will enliven the rest of the month. At Halloween try an action figure theme or safari look for a costume selection. November 1–9 a Mercury transit promises productive travel. Pursue writing or public speaking. Your words are influential during early November. The last three weeks of November accent multitasking and keeping up with current events. Transits in your 3rd house encourage variety and an exchange of ideas.

December ushers in a merry and bright Venus transit. Revel in festive art, seasonal music and literature. Accept invitations to social events or plan your own holiday gathering to honor the Winter Solstice. The Full Moon on December 26 awakens your curiosity about new avenues of learning and other ways of life. On December 31 Jupiter completes its retrograde cycle in your 7th house. A partnership or relationship enters a new phase. January focuses on allowing others the freedom to grow and change while you reexamine the roles associates play in your own life. January 1–13 Mercury influences your sector of finances. Budgeting and planning a business agenda can be important. A decision about transportation, possibly involving a new vehicle, is likely near January 11. The last half of January concerns homelife and living arrangements.

As February begins honor Candlemas by lighting peppermint incense or scented candles dedicated to strengthening family unity. February 5–22 relatives will have much to discuss. Listen carefully. Share your own thoughts to facilitate understanding. The Full Moon on February 24 encourages pursuing a cherished wish. Late February–March 9 Mercury joins the Sun in your 5th house. Enjoy a favorite sport, hobby or other leisure pursuit. A favorable Venus influence spans March 12 to Winter's end. This benefits both romance and finances.

HEALTH
Mercury transits your health sector March 20–April 2 and again June 11–26. Important information regarding health is available. A health challenge can be successfully addressed.

The Full Moon on September 29 favors healing through affirmations and visualization. Connect with a spirit guide or angel at that time to facilitate wellness.

LOVE
It's complicated this year. The eclipses on April 20 and October 28 affect your 7th house of partnership and commitment. A cycle of change and growth affects closest relationships. Love links involve endings or beginnings. All year Saturn is in your 5th house of romance. This encourages a desire for stability in love. The path to happiness is paved with effort or sacrifice. In December Venus transits Scorpio, bringing a turn for the better.

SPIRITUALITY
In Peru's Nazca zodiac Scorpio's sign is the Monkey. This most intelligent and clever of the animal signs is also familiar and friendly—a joker, a trickster. Monkey brings a reminder to be alert and keep learning. Stories and parables offer insight regarding spiritual growth. The eclipse on October 14 in your 12th house promises spiritual awakening, especially through dream interpretation and meditation.

FINANCE
Jupiter and Uranus will oppose your Sun from late May through the Winter. This suggests influences from associates which will affect your finances. Use care in pursuing joint financial ventures if a risk is involved, especially while Jupiter is retrograde September 4–December 31. The late Winter brings a favorable Saturn aspect, making early 2024 promising for financial gain.

SAGITTARIUS
November 22–December 21
Spring 2023–Spring 2024 for those
born under the sign of the Archer

Philosophical and idealistic Sagittarius finds satisfaction in guiding others toward growth. You are a natural leader, teacher or mentor. Your attachment to nature and animals is strong, especially regarding horses and large dogs. Training animals for competitions and sports can be of interest. Your competitive spirit inspires you to play every game to win. Faraway places and other ways of life beckon to you. Your symbol, the Archer, aims his bow and arrow toward ever higher and more distant targets.

Mars completes an opposition to your Sun March 20-24. Spring's earliest days favor resolving differences. Honor the Vernal Equinox with offerings and blessings for peace. A compromise could offer the best route to conflict resolution. During early April Venus brightens your 6th house. A congenial mood makes daily duties more enjoyable. Your employment situation can be improved if you project an upbeat outlook. On May Day offer flowers, plants or other tokens of appreciation to coworkers. The last half of April – May 18 brings a Mars influence in your 8th house. A mystery captivates you. This can involve reincarnation or a connection with the spirit world. From late May throughout July a parade of Fire sign tran-

sits encourages your natural wanderlust and curiosity. A journey to another land or foreign language studies could be highlights. Honor the Summer Solstice with an international themed celebration.

On July 29 Mercury crosses your midheaven. This sets the pace for ideas and information exchanges involving your career aspirations. At Lammas professional studies and travel opportunities materialize. This begins a chain of productivity which sets a busy pace throughout August and September. On September 4 Jupiter turns retrograde in your 6th house. A cycle begins which encourages correcting an unsatisfactory situation. Sift through memories for clues about making the best decisions impacting the here and now. A past pattern repeats and memories offer valuable indicators of what to expect in the times to come. At the Autumnal Equinox focus on how to clarify plans and display your potential. As October begins friends offer invitations and share thoughts about the future. The eclipse on October 14 brings changes in your social circle. A longtime affiliation can be replaced by a new connection. Déjà vu touches All Hallows. Resurrect a favorite costume from yesteryear or assemble vintage garments to create a unique look.

November begins with a desire to retreat and relax. The darkening Autumn days encourage peaceful contemplation. The mood shifts when Mars enters Sagittarius on November 23. This is a dynamic influence, promising a busy pace through the Winter holiday season. On the Winter Solstice release anger or frustration and ignite a yule log or bayberry candle to attract new projects and productivity. On December 31 Jupiter, your ruler, turns direct. Past frustrations and redundant situations become memories. January accents financial considerations. A hobby or creative project could have income generating potential. The first three weeks of January are brightened by a strong Venus influence. Appreciation and admiration come your way. At Candlemas the financial picture is promising. Dedicate green and gold candles for a prosperity ritual.

The first three weeks of February bring a focus on your 3rd house. You will be juggling several projects at once. Scheduling, errands and communication will be important. Get priorities in order. A visit from a neighbor or sibling initiates a revealing conversation near the New Moon on February 9. Late February–March 9 home and family matters will absorb your attention. Discuss ways to make living arrangements more enjoyable for all concerned. Redecorating or remodeling your dwelling could be in your plans. You may feel rather jittery near Leap Day on February 29. Maintain patience with resolving glitches. The final days of Winter bring a celestial pattern which involves Mars and Pluto. Differing opinions and controversial discussions arise. Be fair and tactful in sharing your opinions to preserve valued friendships. Diffuse tension by interjecting a bit of light, kindly humor into conversations.

HEALTH

Confinement of any kind is repugnant to the freedom-loving and adventurous Sagittarian. Space and plenty of fresh air will contribute to your well-being. The hip and leg areas are vulnerable, so be cautious with activities involving potential falls or collisions. Progress in reaching wellness goals can be achieved from the Vernal Equinox through May 15, when Jupiter favorably aspects your Sun. Mars conjoins your Sun from November 24 to January 3. Pace yourself then. Avoid overdoing it with exercise programs or other challenges and risks.

LOVE

The Full Moon in Sagittarius on June 3 shines in your 1st house. You will be at the center of attention. Your upbeat personality is an asset which impresses others. Social and business connections are favored December 30–January 22 when Venus transits Sagittarius. This is promising for attracting happiness in love and romance.

SPIRITUALITY

In Peru's Nazca zodiac the Hummingbird relates to Sagittarius. Throughout the Andes hummingbirds symbolize happiness. Always focus on interests which generate personal happiness to assure spiritual growth. Psychic connections with animal companions also connect with your higher self. The eclipse on May 5 in your 12th house activates spiritual insights.

FINANCE

A Saturn influence in your 4th house all year shows possible financial challenges involving home and property or expenses generated by relatives. The New Moon on January 11 is in your financial sector. That's a good time to make changes in budgeting and financial management.

CAPRICORN

December 22–January 19

Spring 2023–Spring 2024 for those
born under the sign of the Goat

A stable and responsible approach to the journey of life characterizes the zodiac's sure footed climber. The Goat combines a determined, conventional outlook with ambition. Dedicated to moving forward, meeting goals and acquiring success, you are loyal to tradition. Ruled by time-conscious Saturn, Capricorns usually have a great sense of timing. You uphold expectations of having a return on your investments of time, effort and resources. Your sense of humor is clever with subtle irony and hints of sarcasm.

The springtime arrives joyfully, and love is in the air. Venus is in your romance and pleasure sector at the Vernal Equinox. This romantic trend continues until April 10. From late April through May 19 an opposition from Mars generates a competitive spirit. Be diplomatic if involved in partnerships. Dedicate May Day rites to honor peace and tolerance. From late May through June 5 Venus transits your 7th house. Both business and personal relationships will improve. A talented and caring associate is supportive.

In June Saturn turns retrograde in your 3rd house. A vehicle might need replacement or repairs. Address transportation needs. At the Summer Solstice

observances include an affirmation for safe and comfortable travel. Emotions will motivate you at the Full Moon in Capricorn on July 3. Patriotism as well as family life are priorities. From mid-July through August 26 a favorable Mars transit encourages adventure and exploration. Celebrate Lammastide by traveling to a sacred site. August 27 through late October several powerful transits impact your midheaven. A competitive colleague poses a challenge. There is news coming related to your career. Learn about what's new regarding your field of expertise. The eclipse on October 14 can bring a new direction involving your career. Be flexible. Remember that to grow means to change. For All Hallows an earthy costume would be ideal. Consider a Mother Nature or Green Man look. A woodsman, scout or alpine hiker theme would be other good options.

During November your 11th house is highlighted. Heed suggestions offered by friends. Conversations revolve around a long-term wish or goal. From November 9 to early December Venus activates your sector of recognition and achievement. A bonus or award of merit can come your way. Your working environment is cordial and enjoyable. December 1–22 Mercury will transit Capricorn. Meetings and important communication can offer helpful insights. At the Winter Solstice reflect upon messages which arrive. A worthwhile idea comes to mind near the end of the month. Mars is in Capricorn January 3–February 12. This brings a tremendous burst of enthusiasm and energy. An executive position or other challenge can be offered. Pace yourself regarding exercise regimes though. Don't overdo things and become overly tired. The week of the Full Moon on January 25 affects your 8th house. A past life recollection can arise, providing insights into your life path and mission. Late January accents afterlife connections. If a spirit entity makes itself known, the intent is one of friendly concern. At Candlemas light an orange or yellow candle. This encourages spirit attachments to loosen their hold and drift amicably into other dimensions. February 1–15 Venus conjoins your Sun. There is a graceful combination of friendship and business. You will project an attractive appearance. From late February through Winter's end your financial sector is highlighted. There will be opportunities to add to your income. At the same time financial demands can cause some stress. Patience and strategy are important in meeting monetary goals and obligations during February and March. March 10–20 Mercury affects your 4th house. Your thoughts and conversations can revolve around home improvements, possibly a residential move or real estate investments.

HEALTH

Since January of 2008 Pluto has been moving through Capricorn. Since then there have been a series of health-related considerations and adjustments to cope with. This generational influence will be passing on January 20, 2024 when Pluto changes signs. For you this promises a better grasp of health conditions. An ongoing health concern can be resolved this year. The care of your teeth and knees are good places to begin when looking into maintaining wellness.

LOVE

Benevolent Jupiter will transit your love sector from May 17 through the end of the Winter. This long transit points to a nurturing relationship with potential for stability and growth coming into your life. The eclipses on April 20 and October 28 are both in your sector of love and romance. Expect some romantic sparkle and excitement. An old involvement could wane while a new attraction begins near those eclipse dates.

SPIRITUALITY

In Peru's Nazca zodiac the Frigate Bird is Capricorn's spiritual symbol. Frigate birds dwell near tropical oceans, gliding on warm updrafts below the clouds. Purity and honesty are safeguarded by Frigate Bird, who is seen as a kind of winged angel who both brings and takes away luck. July 29–October 4 Mercury makes a long transit which attracts travel and study preferences which can deepen spiritual awareness. The specifics are revealed near the New Moon on September 14.

FINANCE

From late March through April there is potential for profits from real estate dealings, a family fund or businesses linked to antiques and collectibles. When Pluto changes signs in late January it will begin to affect your 2nd house of income. This is a pattern which lasts for many years. Consider how your source of income might be changing. Study the financial trends linked to global economic situations. This indicates how to adjust your personal finances.

AQUARIUS
January 20–February 18
Spring 2023–Spring 2024 for those
born under the sign of the Water Bearer

Aquarius is the sign of nonconformity. The charming and complex Water Bearer is motivated by curiosity. You can amaze and surprise associates, as you so often break away from traditions and past habits. You cherish freedom. Friendship is important, too. You value relationships which are free flowing and fluid. Commitment to a cause or ideal can steer the course of your life. Along with unpredictable Uranus, the planet Saturn co-rules Aquarius. Saturn's influence brings a reminder that Aquarians have an inherent materialistic side and will usually prioritize financial security.

The Vernal Equinox dawns with Saturn beginning a transit of about two and a half years through your financial sector. Include an affirmation for prosperity in a seasonal celebration. Patience is important in regard to generating extra income during the springtime. On March 25 Mars enters your 6th house, an influence which sets the pace until mid May. This brings an urge to improve and organize your daily work environment. A connection with animal companions is especially strong near May Day. Prepare a special treat for a beloved cat, dog, bird or other small pet. The eclipse on May 5 impacts your 10th house. By the end of the month your career focus shifts. Put your best foot forward with colleagues. Your public image and reputation can be scrutinized. In early June Venus joins Mars in your relationship sector. An energetic and talented partner motivates and inspires you. Suggestions are made regarding a commitment or collaboration on an important project. At the Summer Solstice share in blessing common goals. Toast the future at a ritual feast.

July 1–10 Mercury and the Sun impact your health. Select wholesome menu options and other ways for improving wellness. By mid-July Mars highlights your 8th house, setting the pace until August 26. Endings and transformations, rebirth, renewal and mysteries of all kinds will be the focus. A past life recollection and messages from the spirit world can captivate you. The Full Moon in Aquarius coincides with Lammas on August 1. This marks a time of profound realization. Decide to put the past to rest. Dedicate an altar to peace and freedom while honoring the seasonal rites. The second Full Moon in August, on the 30th, is a rare and lucky Blue Moon. It impacts your financial sector and can light the pathway to acquiring greater wealth.

Throughout September and early October Mars will trine your Sun. This brings a burst of energy and enthusiasm. Your sense of adventure as well as your yearning for knowledge will be underscored. Make plans for travel or pursue a course of study near the Autumnal Equinox. October 5–25 a favorable influence from Mercury encourages the expression of thoughts and ideas. You might be drawn into stimulating conversations or write a story or poetry. This is also a wonderful time to seek expert advice. As All Hallows nears you will feel an urge to advocate for vulnerable people or animals. Honor Halloween by participating in a charitable event. A black cat or other animal theme look are suggested costume choices.

During the first three weeks of November several transits indicate a hectic pace. Make time to relax. Resolve differences through compromise. By November 22 camaraderie with cheerful friends will help you to face the future. December 1–4 a trine from Venus favors decorating and wrapping gifts in preparation for the Winter holidays. The 2nd and 3rd weeks of December bring greetings from those who have been out of touch for a while. At the Winter Solstice reflect upon how others are affecting you. Consider stepping back from a friendship you've outgrown or which is a source of angst. January begins with Jupiter completing its retrograde in your zone of home life and real estate. A residential move or home improvement can be planned. A relative's accomplishments are encouraging.

The New Moon on January 11 favors quiet reverie. Contemplate the guidance received from the thoughts and inclinations arising from within. A shopping spree tempts you from late January through Candlemas. Light candles of appreciation to bless the crystals and other possessions you treasure. February 16–March 11 Venus transits Aquarius. This welcomes a happy sparkle into your social life. Winter's finale gathers several transits in your financial sector. A new source of income is revealed. Review your budget to form the best future financial strategy.

HEALTH
Pluto flirts with the Capricorn-Aquarius cusp all year. Preventative health care and analyzing what your body is telling you is a must. You may be especially sensitive to extreme weather and other environmental factors. It's a good time to overcome any negative health habits.

LOVE
A nurturing friendship is often the basis for the growth of true love for Aquarians. Venus, the celestial love goddess, influences love and friendship favorably April 11–May 6 and February 16–March 11.

SPIRITUALITY
The Root, your sacred symbol in the Nazca zodiac, has a unique link to plants. Honoring the growth cycle as well as stability, being rooted, and having a close link with the deep Earth forms your spiritual message. The solar eclipse on October 14 affects your 9th house of philosophy and travel. Near that date a visit to a sacred site or connecting with different belief systems can stimulate spiritual awakening.

FINANCE
Serious Saturn is in your 2nd house of earned income all year. This influence brings worries about finances. Enjoy all you have but live within your means. Patient, conservative financial practices now will promise rewards in the future.

PISCES
February 19 – March 20
Spring 2023 – Spring 2024 for those
born under the sign of the Fish

Sensitive, responsive Pisces easily absorbs the influences of nearby people and places. Cloaked in empathy and compassion, retreating into a dream world appeals to you. Your intuition is well developed. Often this shows genuine psychic and paranormal aptitude. Symbolized by the two fish, tied together yet forever swimming in different directions, this Neptune-ruled birth sign tries to reconcile paradoxes and avoid conflict. Think of a mild clear blue tropical sea, transparent and bejeweled with sunshine connecting with a stormy deep ocean rolling toward a rocky beach. Pisces embraces both of these conflicting images and more.

At the Vernal Equinox the Sun joins Mercury and Jupiter in your 2nd house of money matters. Your thoughts and conversations will revolve around finances late March through mid-April. The New Moon on March 21 is an excellent time for preparing a prosperity blessing and for exploring income-producing opportunities. The eclipse on April 20 shifts your priorities toward travel and current events. On May Day retrograde Mercury favors a reunion and sorting through memorabilia. Venus highlights your sector of love and pleasure from early May through June 4. A vacation

break or other recreational activities are enjoyable. The last three weeks of June finds Mars in your 6th house. The care of beloved animal companions as well as fulfilling a promise can be of concern. This is a good time to get organized and arrange a timetable to address obligations. Relax and meditate at the Summer Solstice. During July and most of August Mars will be in an opposition aspect to your Sun. A lively and competitive spirit is present. Addressing challenges and controversy diplomatically is important. Cooperation and good humor can diffuse tension at Lammastide. Encourage a compromise and discussion over a feast of seasonal fruits and grains.

The Full Blue Moon on August 30 in Pisces brings heightened intuition and insights. A spirit guide's message offers inspiration. This might involve dream interpretation. Throughout September until October 4 a Mercury influence brings distractions and the need to multitask. There is so much happening. Prioritizing can help in coping. Verify appointments and clarify plans during this time. At the Autumnal Equinox everything becomes more manageable. During the first three weeks of October a variety of celestial energies activate your 8th house. Experiences with afterlife contacts offer insights into the eternal mysteries of birth, death and reincarnation. At All Hallows design a costume which reflects a past life or assemble a classical ghostly look. In early to mid November your sector of foreign connections and higher education sets the pace. Travel and study opportunities arise to broaden your perspective. On November 24 Mars begins a transit over your midheaven. This lasts through January 2. Career ambitions are fueled. You will feel motivated to succeed. There can be some competition or controversy among professional contacts near the Winter Solstice. Dedicate seasonal rites to showcasing your brightest and best talents.

January 1–13 Mercury squares your Sun, activating your career sector. There can be mixed feelings about a job situation. You might research new employment opportunities or seek to approach your work from a different vantage point. The New Moon on January 11 is in your sector of wishes and future aspirations. Define your goals. During the last half of January Jupiter and Uranus will impact your 3rd house. Communication glitches can be resolved. There might be significant interaction with neighbors then. Possibly a neighborhood watch group or social event will be organized. On January 25 the Full Moon highlights your health sector, bringing fitness factors to attention. At Candlemas light scented votive candles, honoring your body as the temple of the spirit. Throughout February several planets activate your 12th house. You will feel an urge to retreat and cherish moments of peace and privacy. On March 12 Venus enters Pisces. Winter's final days promise happiness through relationships of all kinds. Pursue social and artistic interests.

HEALTH

Saturn will transit Pisces all year long, impacting your 1st house. Pay attention to wellness factors. A wholesome diet, enough rest and nurturing activities will help in coping with health concerns.

Neptune, your ruler, will be retrograde from July 1 to December 6. That time span can reveal any health situations stemming from old habits or other challenges. Always pay attention to the health and comfort of your feet. Reflexology and comfortable footwear can do much to add to your overall well-being.

LOVE

Visits to the waterfront, tours of aquariums or historic sites provide favorable backdrops for romantic interludes. May and early June find Venus transiting your 5th house of love and pleasure. This promises romantic bliss. December brings another favorable Venus transit. During the Winter holiday season socialize and nurture love. The Full Moon on December 26 brightens and heightens a love connection.

SPIRITUALITY

The Fish is your symbol in both the familiar Western zodiac and the Nazca zodiac. In Peru's great desert, Fish is the revered spirit of the water. Water renews life after a drought. Preserving and honoring the life breath is your spiritual mission. The eclipse on May 5 affects your sector of philosophy and travel. Spiritual awakening is very likely at that time. Pursue spiritual studies. Consider arranging a visit to a sacred site.

FINANCE

From the Vernal Equinox until May 16 Jupiter blesses your 2nd house of money. Cultivate income-producing opportunities at that time and set a profitable and solid financial direction for the future. Saturn's influence in Pisces this year rewards patience and dedication.

Sites of Awe

The Rollright Stones

IT'S ENGLAND...so it is lightly raining. In the US we call it drizzling. I've put the postal code into the GPS but it looks like it brought me to an open field with a lot of sheep!

I've read about the prehistoric Rollright Stones over the years. They include the King's Men—a circle of stones over 100 feet in diameter with 77 stones marking out the circle, the Whispering Knights—a grouping of stones enclosed by a circular fence and thought to be the earliest of the stone groupings and the King Stone—one lone upright stone measuring over seven feet tall and located just over 200 feet northeast of the King's Men.

Some believe the magnificent stones to be grave markers, some believe them to be places of power located on ley lines and others believe these locations to be land markers indicating prehistoric trading sites. I believe in the folklore tales of the Witch who turned a King and his Knights into stones and then became an elder tree to stand guard nearby and watch over them.

It is common knowledge that many Pagans and Witches have visited this site over the years for amusement and to perform ritual. Some notable such pilgrims include William Gray, the Regency, the Bricket Wood Coven and other Gardnerian groups.

Oh, here I am chattering to my friends in the car and I almost missed a turn! The sign says, "Little Rollright." I hope this is correct because Greater Rollright was definitely wrong. Generally these postal codes are quite accurate, but in this case, I should have brought a pendulum along.

Worn path inside the stones.

There are a couple of cars parked on the left (of course they are, we are in the UK!) Looks like an opening in the hedge and a small green sign. I'll park here. Walking up to the sign I see a cattle gate. These are handy things that keep grazing animals on one side while people can pass through. It is an ingenious country invention that would probably take a team of engineers to figure out today.

Yup, this is the right place. There is a small fee requested as a donation to the Rollright Trust. I am so very excited to be here—I have been wanting to come here for decades! Many years ago when I was in New York City, I was visiting the Weiser bookshop on lower Broadway. Donald Weiser recommended a book to me called *The Rollright Ritual* by William Gray. I purchased it and to my amazement, it was autographed! Since reading it, I have always

wanted to come here. I feel my heart racing with excitement and a nervous anticipation of the feeling of natural power to come.

Going down this short path, the space is now opening up and to my right are the King's Men! I'm impressed—very awe-struck by the natural beauty and prehistoric feeling of power that this circle exudes. I don't know what to do first. I'm walking around the outside because it almost feels as if crossing over into the space is like crossing over a cast ritual circle. At first finding myself at the East of the stone circle, I'm automatically moving clockwise to the South. Touching the stones is such a pleasure. There is a beautiful combination of age and steadfastness to them. Over time, this seems to have been flavored by the visitors. I can hear whispers of the people who have come before me and walked

Hag stones.

this same path. Several of these large stones have holes in them clear through—almost like a three-foot hagstone. Can't wear this around my neck! But leaning over, I can't help but whisper through the hole to ask the fairy custodians of this fine and sacred site for a small gift. Now I dig through my bag to find a gift to leave in exchange. Placing the gift is going to require some thought and intuition. There are small gifts all over the stones and the ground beneath them—coins, food, shells, feathers, jewelry, ribbons, notes, flowers, crystals and more.

Wow, over here in the West there are clootie trees! They're adorned with a variety of ribbons, many showing age from fading and having the wind tear them apart. Maybe the local birds are using threads for their nests, too. Hopefully these ribbons

are made of natural materials. I remember the Rollright Trust putting out a statement or something talking about ritual litter and items being left behind that do not degrade naturally. I'm looking through my bag for a small piece of fabric, but not having any luck. It is important that I make an offering because someone I love isn't feeling well and I want to ask for good heath in return. Ok, I'll tear a strip of fabric from my shirt. Red is not the color I would have chosen, but I'll concentrate on it bringing nutrients through his blood to the parts of the mind and body that need it most. There, this makes me feel good. And a strong gust of wind has just picked up as if in acceptance of the offering. The wind seems to only be blowing through this one tree—gotta love the spirits! They communicate very succinctly if you know how to listen.

Moving along to the North, it feels quite different from the other quarters—almost as if it were more "physical" in some way. The other directions seemed more "elemental" in their nature. Maybe it is because the North is closest to the road. Many of these old sites will lose some power or become more trapped against the physical world over time. But I have found that if the visitor numbers decrease and the areas are left to their own devices, they usually regenerate their power. I believe this is because many of them are on sacred ground that releases energy which in turn causes the land above it to draw the sacredness to it, bringing the holy stones, wells, groves and shrines to come to rest there.

Well now I've made offerings to the stones and land, also to the clootie trees. I've completed my path around the stones, inside and outside the ring. I've also taken pictures that I will submit to The Witches' Almanac along with this article. I want the reader to see things exactly as I did. So, dear reader, look at the photos with your "magic eyes" and see if you can see a fairy or two. My travel companions are waiting for me at the path—time to walk back toward the car, cross the street and walk to the King's Stone which is very close. Then back to the car to drive on to the Whispering Knights, which I believe is down the street a bit.

I've changed my mind. As I started down the path several things are coming to mind—I only made two offerings (I like threes,) I didn't see an elder tree representing the Witch that stands guard, I didn't do any form

Clootie trees.

The King Stone

of ritual to truly connect me with this sacred site. I always like to end a visit with some form of ritual so that I carry not only the memory of the site, but a bit of its spirituality home with me. Then my memories can form in layers in my mind. Ok, back I go.

I'm going to the center of the circle to meditate a bit first. Oh, no need to meditate, I'm finding myself drawn to a different place. Facing East, I'm making my personal offering here in the center of the circle. Everything is changing. Things seem misty or blurred. I don't know what is happening but I guess I will just stand here and wait. Without moving, I'm seeing my hands in front of me, placed on the ground. I'm crouched down and looking at the grass-covered ground in front of me. Looking up, there before me, just outside the circle in the East, is the biggest elder tree I've ever seen. Far beyond the size that an elder tree can grow to, it is

a phantasmic elder tree in Fairy! I've crossed. Walking up to the tree, I'm moved to hold my hand out. A tiny twig falls from a branch into my hand and I turn and go back to the center of the circle, so very grateful. Once again I find myself with my hands on the ground, clutching a tiny twig, and the world around me is sharp and clear again.

I am blessed. For a brief moment, I have been given a glimpse into Fairy and a gift to return with.

Later:

I hesitated about writing this detail for a book, wanting to keep it to myself. But I feel as if there is someone out there who needs to see that these things are more real than the "real" that you are taught. "Real" comes from within.

If you are ever fortunate enough to visit the Rollright Stones, you can reach out to the Rollright Trust. Should you choose to ask, they will allow you to book a time to use the site—even to perform rituals! Imagine a romantic late-night ritual under a full Moon at the gate of Fairy.

—ARMAND TABER

184

THE EPITAPH OF
BENJAMIN FRANKLIN

The Body

of

B. Franklin, Printer

Like the Cover of an old Booke

Its Contents torn out

And Stript of its Lettering and Gilding

Lies here Food for the worms.

Yet the Work Shall not be lost

For it will (as he believ'd) appear once more,

In a new + most beautiful Edition,

Corrected + amended,

By

The Author.

—Written for himself, 1728

Reviews

New World Witchery; A Trove of North American Folk Magic
Cory Thomas Hutcheson
ISBN-13: 978-0738762128
Llewellyn Publications
$27.99

SEVERAL THINGS set *New World Witchery* apart from other books on North American magical traditions. Firstly, it opens by explicitly rejecting mythologized images of Witches, suggesting that friends, neighbors and loved ones more likely fit the description. Secondly, it is simultaneously reliably researched and intended to instruct actual magical practice. Lastly, it presents a broad range of North American magical traditions and does not treat the Mason-Dixon line as some kind of entry point into Fairyland. (Perhaps regretfully, the American South is not a mystical region awash in root-doctoring magical grandmothers.) Hutcheson does occasionally exoticize both the South and Appalachia, but does not completely fall into the trope. In fact, reading this book leads you to believe that the author has actually visited these regions— something that cannot be said for many similar texts.

Hutcheson's work incorporates magic from many regions and traditions including power doctors, granny women, root working, *brujeria* and folk traditions of the mid-Atlantic and New England, among others. He writes about materials and practices such as dollies, herbs, dousing, divination and spirit flight and does not shy away from subjects like meeting the devil at the crossroads that might challenge readers but nonetheless remain important aspects of some forms of magic in North America. Throughout the book, you feel as though the information is being presented in a straightforward manner appropriate to the topic.

The author holds a doctorate in American Studies, but the book does not read a bit like an academic tome! It is a practical text—it contextualizes specific practices by discussing their folklore and history while also including copious information on how to go about doing them. His "Dirt Under the Nails" sections in each chapter provide explicit instructions for making floor washes and sweetening jars, setting lights, meeting the Man in Black and many other charms, formulae and practices. He follows these up with a section on "The Work" which provides spiritual exercises the reader can engage in to deepen their understanding and connection to their magic. Anyone interested in learning about or practicing any form of North American magic would do well to select *New World Witchery.*

Lights, Camera, Witchcraft; A Critical History of Witches in American Film and Television
Heather Greene
ISBN-13: 978-0738768533
Llewellyn Publications
$29.99

MORTICIA ADDAMS, Sabrina Spellman, Queen Elsa of Arendelle. These women of television and film, of camp, horror and fantasy, bear so little resemblance to the she-devils of the *Malleus Maleficarum* that they must surely be different sorts of creatures than the victims of the Salem. But are they really so different? Little girls wear tiaras and Elsa-themed backpacks because they desire power and beauty. Sabrina's appeal is inseparable from her diabolical display of teenage female sexuality. The great crime and great enticement of these characters boils down to each being, as Greene puts it, "the woman who knows too much," precisely what historic persecutors of Witchcraft feared.

Lights, Camera, Witchcraft; A Critical History of Witches in American Film and Television traces the figure of the Witch from her role as a non-defining element of a story based in fairy tale to being the major character. Heather Greene deftly connects each development in film and storytelling to corresponding developments in culture and society. The silver screen is, after all, the collective fantasy of a culture writ large and to understand it is to understand the society that produced it.

The comprehensive text is organized chronologically, beginning with the dawning influence of film in the late 19th century. It follows the changing representations of the Witch through the green face Wicked Witch, the housewife charmers, the satanic depictions of the 80s and through to the films and TV series of 2020. Each section is accompanied by meaningful, in-depth analysis based in feminism and filmography. For the film buff, the fascinated watcher or the real-life Witch, Heather Greene's thoughtful and thorough work is a must-read. Deride her, fear her or laud her, the Witch enchants all her viewers.

Fire Magic (Elements of Witchcraft, 3)
Josephine Winter
ISBN-13: 978-0738763736
Llewellyn Publications
$17.99

IN THE introduction to Josephine Winter's *Fire Magic,* she reflects on the central role that Fire plays in human ritual life: from bonfires to candles, Fire often features prominently in magical and religious practices the world over. However, *Fire Magic* is much more than an account of the element as an abstract concept—it is a thorough exploration of Fire in both its symbolic and physical forms in the roles it plays in religion, magic and daily life.

The early chapters of Winter's book provide a fascinating overview of the history, folklore and mythology of Fire as found in many different cultures. Her research is detailed but the writing remains light and approachable. She often sites primary texts and while she is quick to note where historical understanding differs from more contemporary interpretations, she has a refreshing way of dismissing neither. For example, her section on the Goddess Cerridwen focusses primarily on her role in Welsh mythology while also addressing her more modern representation as a crone Goddess without rejecting either.

The latter two-thirds of the book delivers a wealth of information about the element of Fire as it relates to magical practice. Winter provides chapters dedicated to herbs, crystals, animals, astrological and tarot symbolism and more. Each of these sections offers detailed and illuminating information. The rituals, spells and recipes that close out the book draw on the information presented earlier and provide practical, readily usable resources for both new and experienced practitioners to draw on.

This volume is part of a larger series on the Elements published by Llewellyn Books. However, whether you intend to purchase the other books in the series or not, this volume certainly stands up as a work of its own. Winter's insights and research are sure to be a valuable addition to your bookshelf.

The Poison Path Herbal; Baneful Herbs, Medicinal Nightshades & Ritual Entheogens
Coby Michael, Park Street Press
ISBN-13: 978-1644113349
Park Street Press
$19.99

ONE OF THE primary ways to deepen your Pagan or Witch spirituality is to find ways to interact magically with the world around you. Working with plants is one of the most readily available methods for doing so, but can feel inaccessible as there is little reliable published information on how to use most of the plants traditionally associated with Witchcraft. In *The Poison Path Herbal*, Coby Michael provides the thorough guidance needed to begin working with entheogenic and baneful plants in your Witchcraft.

The book is divided into three sections. The first defines what the poison path is and discusses the traditional roles of entheogens in Witchcraft and the role of poisonous plants in baneful magic. It also includes scientific information about the chemical compounds found in these plants and how they impact the body. The second section is divided into chapters on plants associated with Saturn, Venus and Mercury, as most all poisonous plants fall under the domain of one of these three planetary energies. Moreover, these planets and their associated deities represent three distinct ways of using entheogenic plants for magic. The third section includes instructions and formulas for compounding plants and using them magically, and provides information on how to grow each from seed.

Recipes that can kill you are easily found, while instructions on how to use them meaningfully and magically are hard to come by. What truly sets *The Poison Path Herbal* apart is that each section explores the classical mythology of these plants as well presenting traditional uses, scientific information and useful tips gleaned from the author's personal experience. Even Witches who never intend to work with these plants in traditional ways will appreciate the treasure trove of lore Coby Michael has gathered. Whether you buy it just for information or to augment your path by working directly with baneful plants, *The Poison Path Herbal* deserves a place on every serious practitioner's shelf.

The Last Ecstasy of Life; Celtic Mysteries of Death and Dying
Phyllida Anam-Áire
ISBN-13: 978-1644112656
Findhorn Press
$14.93

THE REALITY of death is one that all people face at some point. While there are many books exploring the topic of death and dying, few written from a Pagan perspective are as thoughtful and complete as Phyllida Anam-Áire's *The Last Ecstasy of Life*. Anam-Áire brings a wealth of personal and professional experience to her understanding of death. In addition to being a psychotherapist—she was a student of Dr. Elisabeth Kübler-Ross, the psychiatrist who outlined the five stages of grief—Anam-Áire is an experienced follower of Celtic mysteries, a former Catholic nun, a poet and a musician. Above all she brings her own keen spiritual observations about the dying process.

Anam-Áire reflects on dying not as a moment of ending but as a sacred act of Spirit releasing itself from Ego. This is not only a book of theory, however. Interspersed throughout the reader will find poems, meditations, and visualizations that provide important spiritual tools for the dying as well as those who spending time with the dying. In doing so she provides a detailed road map to the transformations that come with death and grief, providing not only philosophical insight but also practical guidance for the journey.

In her close examination of the dying process, Anam-Áire makes ample use of her background in therapy. She provides counsel to those grieving through family conflict, struggling with past hurts or facing emotionally difficult tasks like supporting a friend through the death of a child. Although the subject matter is profound, Anam-Áire writes with a conversational style that makes it approachable and the format invites reflection, giving ample space for readers to contemplate their own thoughts and experiences.

While Anam-Áire writes unashamedly from her own Celtic background, *The Last Ecstasy of Life* will prove valuable to followers of many different paths as well as those who are just spiritually inclined. Death touches the lives of everyone and it helps to have a wise and experienced guide who has thought deeply about it. Anam-Áire offers herself as just such a guide through this book—it will be well worth your time to take her up on the offer.

From a Witch's Mailbox

A name by any other name

Why do people take a new name in the Craft and should I?—Submitted by Seana Maxwell

The taking of a new name is not uncommon for those entering a new religion or refocusing their dedication and attention. The taking of a new name in the Craft is done for a few reasons. The number one reason that most will point to is that the new name is becoming visible to the community and signals to some extent the aspirations of the new member. Another reason for a new name is for the creation of a "magical persona." The newly chosen name, in this case, is only used in magical situations and is rarely known outside your immediate Craft family and close associates. Not all magical communities require that you take a new name. Some might require that you have a magical motto that you live. In this case the motto is abbreviated in some way so that it may be used as a name. In either case, the taking of a name or motto is a task that should not be approached lightly. Do your research before taking on a new name—it can greatly affect your life. A good place to start in the case of a name is mythology. A caution given to many is that you want to be careful to not choose a name or motto that is too big. You should have room to realistically grow with the name.

I magic, therefore I am

Is okay to do magic for myself or should I ask someone else to do it?—Submitted by Anna Coss

It is very much okay to use magic for yourself. In fact, many begin their foray into Witchcraft and Ceremonial Magic in order to help move things along in their lives. That being said, doing magic should not be a substitute for hard work to achieve your goals in life. Magic is there to make possibilities materialize and give the extra push that may be needed in a given situation. For example, if you are in need of employment, having not been employed for a bit, magic can definitely help improve the odds of getting the job that you want. You will still have to do the job search, send out your resume and do common sense follow up after an interview. It's magic that you are doing, not performing miracles. Having others do magic for you is good when you feel you are too emotionally entangled to think straight. In either case, get to it—do the magic.

This house is now clean

I am moving into a new house, how do I clean it of past energies?—Submitted by Emma Pabon

Well there are as many methods of psychically cleaning a home as there are days in the year. Let's start with the obvious. When you get the new home, if you can have a day or so before the actual move, you are going to be ahead of the game. Regardless of how the home was left by

the previous occupant, you will want to do a regular elbow grease and grit cleaning. Make sure to rid the house literally of the cobwebs and the dust in the corners of each room. If the home has an attic and/or a basement, make sure to get these clean as well. In some ways, they can be worse than the rooms that are lived in! Having the physical cleaning out of the way, you can focus on the psychic energies that may be in the home. Mopping the floors with an herbal infusion is one of the best ways to magically cleanse. The best herbs for this purpose are hyssop and chamomile. To make a floor wash of these, brew a very strong infusion or tea from these herbs. You can then add some of the liquid to a pail full of water and carefully mop each floor with it. After the floors have been cleaned with the infusion, you might want to also clean the very air of each room. Many will smudge with sage. If sage is not appealing, you might want to burn some frankincense. The last part of cleaning a home is to actually protect the home. Using salt water, make an invoking Earth pentagram on each door and each window in the home. All of these can and should be done on a regular basis. It's just good psychic hygiene. There are certainly other ways to clean a home—you might want to do some research and add to these protocols, making them your own.

Feet on the ground

After ritual I often feel very disconnected, is this normal?—Submitted by Derrick Ash

Ritual has different effects on different people. I would first advise that if you are part of a group that you first check in with the group leader or other members of the group. We in many ways seek an altered state when performing ritual. Unless the intention is to "channel" a deity or spirit, you don't want to be totally disconnected. This is especially true if you are doing solitary rituals. Only you can judge how "ecstatic" you can be before it becomes problematic. Some breathing exercises and feeling a connection with the Earth through your feet will help keep you a bit grounded during ritual. After ritual, a good glass of cold water and a light meal will bring you back to the here and now.

Let us hear from you, too

We love to hear from our readers. Letters should be sent with the writer's name (or just first name or initials), address, daytime phone number and email address, if available. Published material may be edited for clarity or length. All letters and emails will become the property of The Witches' Almanac Ltd. *and will not be returned. We regret that due to the volume of correspondence we cannot reply to all communications.*

The Witches' Almanac, Ltd.
P.O. Box 25239
Providence, RI 02905-7700
info@TheWitchesAlmanac.com
www.TheWitchesAlmanac.com

The products and services offered above are paid advertisements.

Discover a Mythical Mystical Realm of
Books, Incense, Candles, Crystals, Oils, Tarot,
Gemstone & Symbolic Jewelry, Statuary, Talismans,
Oracles, Pendulums, Runes, Clothing
& All Things Rare & Magickal...

Avalon

All Things Rare & Magickal

Classes - Events - Psychic Readings
Spiritual Consultaions & Candle Dressing

AVALONBEYOND.COM

1211 Hillcrest St. Orlando Florida 32803 407 895 7439

-Over 20 Years of Magickal Service -

The products and services offered above are paid advertisements.

INTRODUCING

The Weiser Tarot

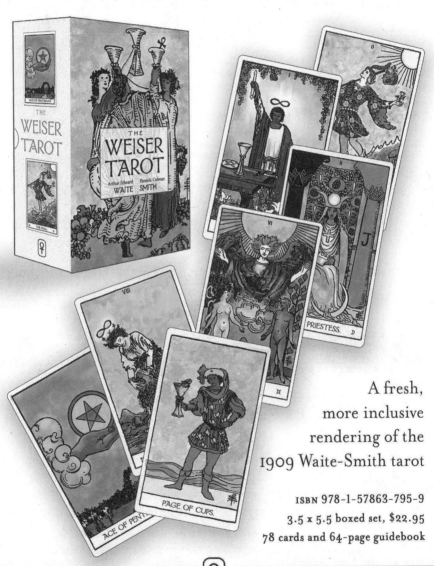

A fresh,
more inclusive
rendering of the
1909 Waite-Smith tarot

ISBN 978-1-57863-795-9
3.5 x 5.5 boxed set, $22.95
78 cards and 64-page guidebook

WEISER BOOKS

800.423.7087   orders@rwwbooks.com

❧MARKETPLACE❧

TO: The Witches' Almanac
P.O. Box 1292, Newport, RI 02840-9998
www.TheWitchesAlmanac.com

Email (required) _____

Name_____

Address_____

City_____ State_____ Zip_____

WITCHCRAFT being by nature one of the secretive arts, it may not be as easy to find us next year. If you'd like to make sure we know where you are, why don't you send us your name, email address and street address? You will certainly hear from us.

≈MARKETPLACE ≈

Dikki-Jo Mullen

The Witches' Almanac Astrologer
skymaiden@juno.com
Sky Maiden Musings dikkijomullen.wordpress.com
Star Dates Astrology Forecasts facebook.com/dikkijo.mullen
Dikki Jo Mullen on **YouTube**

**Seminars, Presentations,
Convention Programs**

Complete Astrology & Parapsychology Services

Paranormal Investigations

*(see the website for astrology articles
and information about upcoming events)*

The Witches' Almanac 2023 Wall Calendar

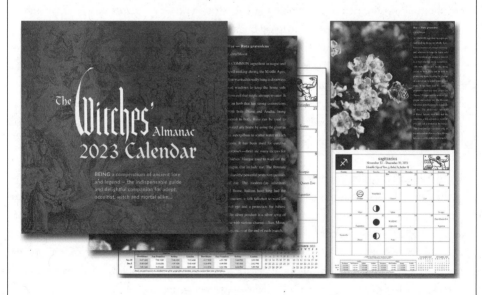

The ever popular Moon Calendar in each issue of The Witches' Almanac is a wall calendar as well. Providing the standard Moon phases, channeled actions and an expanded version of the topic featured in the Moon Calendar are now available in a full-size wall calendar.

Liber Spirituum

BEING A TRUE AND FAITHFUL REPRODUCTION OF
THE GRIMOIRE OF PAUL HUSON

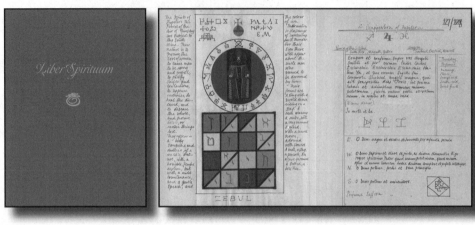

In 1966, as an apprentice mage, Paul Huson began the work of constructing his personal *Liber Spirituum* or *Book of Spirits*. The origins of his work in fact have their genesis a number of years before he took up the pen to illuminate the pages of his *Book of Spirits*. It was in his tender youth that Paul's interest in matters magical began. It was his insatiable curiosity and thirst for knowledge that would eventually lead him to knock on the doors of Dion Fortune's Society of the Inner Light in 1964, as well as studying the practices of the Hermetic Order of the Golden Dawn and the Stella Matutina under the aegis of Israel Regardie. Drawing on this wellspring of knowledge and such venerable works as the *Key of Solomon*, *The Magus*, *Heptameron*, *Three Books of Occult Philosophy* as well as others set down a unique and informed set of rituals, in addition to employing his own artistry in the creation of distinctive imagery.

Using the highest quality photographic reproduction and printing methods, Paul's personal grimoire has here been faithfully and accurately reproduced for the first time. In addition to preserving the ink quality and use of gold and silver paint, this facsimile reproduction has maintained all of Huson's corrections, including torn, pasted, missing pages and his hand drawn and renumbered folios. Preserved as well are the unique characteristics of the original grimoire paper as it has aged through the decades. In this way, the publisher has stayed true to Paul Huson's *Book of Spirits* as it was originally drawn and painted.

223 Pages
Paperback — $59.95
Hardbound in slipcase — $149.95

For further imformation visit: TheWitchesAlmanac.com

MAGIC
An Occult Primer
50 YEAR ANNIVERSARY EDITION
David Conway

The Witches' Almanac presents:

- *A clear, articulate presentation of magic in a workable format*
- *Updated text, graphics and appendices*
- *Foreword by Colin Wilson*

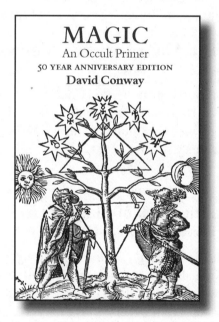

David Conway's *Magic: An Occult Primer* is a seminal work that brought magical training to the every-magician in the early 70s. David is an articulate writer presenting the mysteries in a very workable manner for the serious student. Along with the updated texts on philosophy and practical magic is a plethora of graphics that have all been redrawn, promising to be another collector's edition published by The Witches' Almanac.

384 pages — $24.95

For further information visit TheWitchesAlmanac.com

Aradia
Gospel of the Witches
Charles Godfrey Leland

ARADIA IS THE FIRST work in English in which witchcraft is portrayed as an underground old religion, surviving in secret from ancient Pagan times.

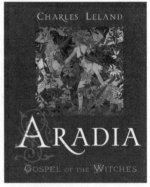

- Used as a core text by many modern Neo-Pagans.
- Foundation material containing traditional witchcraft practices
- This special edition features appreciations by such authors as Paul Huson, Raven Grimassi, Judika Illes, Michael Howard, Christopher Penczak, Myth Woodling, Christina Oakley Harrington, Patricia Della-Piana, Jimahl di Fiosa and Donald Weiser. A beautiful and compelling work, this edition is an up to date format, while keeping the text unchanged. 172 pages $16.95

The ABC of Magic Charms
Elizabeth Pepper

Mankind has sought protection from mysterious forces beyond mortal control. Humans have sought the help of animal, mineral, vegetable. The enlarged edition of *Magic Charms from A to Z*, guides us in calling on these forces. $12.95

The Little Book of Magical Creatures
Elizabeth Pepper and Barbara Stacy

AN UPDATE of the classic *Magical Creatures*, featuring Animals Tame, Animals Wild, Animals Fabulous—plus an added section of enchanting animal myths from other times, other places. *A must for all animal lovers.* $12.95

The Witchcraft of Dame Darrel of York
Charles Godfrey Leland, Introduction by Robert Mathiesen

A beautifully reproduced facsimile of the illuminated manuscript shedding light on the basis for a modern practice. A treasured by those practicing Pagans, as well as scholars. Standard Hardcover $65.00 or Exclusive full leather bound, numbered and slipcased edition $145.00

DAME FORTUNE'S WHEEL TAROT: A PICTORIAL KEY
Paul Huson

Based upon Paul Huson's research in *Mystical Origins of the Tarot, Dame Fortune's Wheel Tarot* illustrates for the first time the earliest, traditional Tarot card interpretations as collected in the 1700s by Jean-Baptiste Alliette. In addition to detailed descriptions, full color reproductions of Huson's original designs for all 79 cards.

WITCHES ALL

A Treasury from past editions, is a collection from *The Witches' Almanac* publications of the past. Arranged by topics, the book, like the popular almanacs, is thought provoking and often spurs the reader on to a tangent leading to even greater discovery. It's perfect for study or casual reading,

GREEK GODS IN LOVE

Barbara Stacy casts a marvelously original eye on the beloved stories of Greek deities, replete with amorous oddities and escapades. We relish these tales in all their splendor and antic humor, and offer an inspired storyteller's fresh version of the old, old mythical magic.

MAGIC CHARMS FROM A TO Z

A treasury of amulets, talismans, fetishes and other lucky objects compiled by the staff of *The Witches' Almanac*. An invaluable guide for all who respond to the call of mystery and enchantment.

LOVE CHARMS

Love has many forms, many aspects. Ceremonies performed in witchcraft celebrate the joy and the blessings of love. Here is a collection of love charms to use now and ever after.

MAGICAL CREATURES

Mystic tradition grants pride of place to many members of the animal kingdom. Some share our life. Others live wild and free. Still others never lived at all, springing instead from the remarkable power of human imagination.

ANCIENT ROMAN HOLIDAYS

The glory that was Rome awaits you in Barbara Stacy's classic presentation of a festive year in Pagan times. Here are the gods and goddesses as the Romans conceived them, accompanied by the annual rites performed in their worship. Scholarly, lighthearted – a rare combination.

CELTIC TREE MAGIC

Robert Graves in *The White Goddess* writes of the significance of trees in the old Celtic lore. *Celtic Tree Magic* is an investigation of the sacred trees in the remarkable Beth-Luis-Nion alphabet and their role in folklore, poetry and mysticism.

MOON LORE

As both the largest and the brightest object in the night sky, and the only one to appear in phases, the Moon has been a rich source of myth for as long as there have been mythmakers.

MAGIC SPELLS
AND INCANTATIONS

Words have magic power. Their sound, spoken or sung, has ever been a part of mystic ritual. From ancient Egypt to the present, those who practice the art of enchantment have drawn inspiration from a treasury of thoughts and themes passed down through the ages.

LOVE FEASTS

Creating meals to share with the one you love can be a sacred ceremony in itself. With the Witch in mind, culinary adept Christine Fox offers magical menus and recipes for every month in the year.

RANDOM RECOLLECTIONS
II, III, IV

Pages culled from the original (no longer available) issues of *The Witches' Almanac*, published annually throughout the 1970s, are now available in a series of tasteful booklets. A treasure for those who missed us the first time around, keepsakes for those who remember.

ORDER FORM

Each timeless edition of *The Witches' Almanac* is unique.
Limited numbers of previous years' editions are available.

Item	Price	Qty.	Total
2023-2024 The Witches' Almanac – Earth: Origin of Chthonic Powers	$13.95		
2022-2023 The Witches' Almanac – The Moon: Transforming the Inner Spirit	$12.95		
2021-2022 The Witches' Almanac – The Sun: Rays of Hope	$12.95		
2020-2021 The Witches' Almanac – Stones: The Foundation of Earth	$12.95		
2019-2020 The Witches' Almanac – Animals: Friends & Familiars	$12.95		
2018-2019 The Witches' Almanac – The Magic of Plants	$12.95		
2017-2018 The Witches' Almanac – Water: Our Primal Source	$12.95		
2016-2017 The Witches' Almanac – Air: the Breath of Life	$12.95		
2014-2015 The Witches' Almanac – Mystic Earth	$12.95		
2013-2014 The Witches' Almanac – Wisdom of the Moon	$11.95		
2012-2013 The Witches' Almanac – Radiance of the Sun	$11.95		
2011-2012 The Witches' Almanac – Stones, Powers of Earth	$11.95		
2010-2011 The Witches' Almanac – Animals Great & Small	$11.95		
2009-2010 The Witches' Almanac – Plants & Healing Herbs	$11.95		
2008-2009 The Witches' Almanac – Divination & Prophecy	$10.95		
2007-2008 The Witches' Almanac – The Element of Water	$9.95		
2003, 2004, 2005, 2006 issues of The Witches' Almanac	$8.95		
1999, 2000, 2001, 2002 issues of The Witches' Almanac	$7.95		
1995, 1996, 1997, 1998 issues of The Witches' Almanac	$6.95		
1993, 1994 issues of The Witches' Almanac	$5.95		
The Witches' Almanac 50 Year Anniversary Edition, paperback	$15.95		
The Witches' Almanac 50 Year Anniversary Edition, hardbound	$24.95		
2023-2024 The Witches' Almanac Wall Calendar	$14.95		
SALE: Bundle I—8 Almanac back issues (1991, 1993–1999) with free book bag	$50.00		
Bundle II—10 Almanac back issues (2000–2009) with free book bag	$65.00		
Bundle III—10 Almanac back issues (2010–2019) with free book bag	$100.00		
Bundle IV—30 Almanac back issues (1993–2022) with free book bag	$215.00		
Liber Spirituum—The Grimoire of Paul Huson, paperback	$59.95		
Liber Spirituum—The Grimoire of Paul Huson, hardbound in slipcase	$149.95		
Dame Fortune's Wheel Tarot: A Pictorial Key	$19.95		
Magic: An Occult Primer—50 Year Anniversary Edition, paperback	$24.95		
Magic: An Occult Primer—50 Year Anniversary Edition, hardbound	$29.95		
The Witches' Almanac Coloring Book	$12.00		
The Witchcraft of Dame Darrel of York, clothbound, signed and numbered, in slip case	$85.00		
The Witchcraft of Dame Darrel of York, leatherbound, signed and numbered, in slip case	$145.00		
Aradia or The Gospel of the Witches	$16.95		
The Horned Shepherd	$16.95		
The ABC of Magic Charms	$12.95		
The Little Book of Magical Creatures	$12.95		

Item	Price	Qty.	Total
Greek Gods in Love	$15.95		
Witches All	$13.95		
Ancient Roman Holidays	$6.95		
Celtic Tree Magic	$7.95		
Love Charms	$6.95		
Love Feasts	$6.95		
Magic Charms from A to Z	$12.95		
Magical Creatures	$12.95		
Magic Spells and Incantations	$12.95		
Moon Lore	$7.95		
Random Recollections III or IV (circle your choices)	$3.95		
The Rede of the Wiccae – Hardcover	$49.95		
The Rede of the Wiccae – Softcover	$22.95		
Keepers of the Flame	$20.95		
Sounds of Infinity	$24.95		
The Magic of Herbs	$24.95		
Harry M. Hyatt's Works on Hoodoo and Folklore: A Full Reprint in 13 Volumes (including audio download) *Hoodoo—Conjuration—Witchcraft—Rootwork* Single volumes are also available starting at $120	$1,400.00		
Subtotal			
Tax (7% sales tax for RI customers)			
Shipping & Handling (See shipping rates section)			
TOTAL			

MISCELLANY			
Item	**Price**	**QTY.**	**Total**
Sterling Silver Colophon	$35.00		
Pouch	$3.95		
Skull Scarf	$20.00		
Natural/Black Book Bag	$17.95		
Red/Black Book Bag	$17.95		
Hooded Sweatshirt, Blk	$30.00		
Hooded Sweatshirt, Red	$30.00		
L-Sleeve T, Black	$15.00		
L-Sleeve T, Red	$15.00		
S-Sleeve T, Black/W	$15.00		

MISCELLANY			
Item	**Price**	**QTY.**	**Total**
S-Sleeve T, Black/R	$15.00		
S-Sleeve T, Dk H/R	$15.00		
S-Sleeve T, Dk H/W	$15.00		
S-Sleeve T, Red/B	$15.00		
S-Sleeve T, Ash/R	$15.00		
S-Sleeve T, Purple/W	$15.00		
Magnets – set of 3	$1.50		
Subtotal			
Tax (7% for RI Customers)			
Shipping and Handling (call for estimate)			
Total			

Payment available by check or money order payable in U. S. funds or credit card or PayPal

The Witches' Almanac, Ltd., PO Box 25239, Providence, RI 02905-7700

(401) 847-3388 (phone) • (888) 897-3388 (fax)
Email: info@TheWitchesAlmanac.com • www.TheWitchesAlmanac.com